Geography 2

*Foundation Skills
for 11-14 year olds*

Clifford Lines MSc

formerly Assistant Director,
East Sussex College of Higher Education

Laurie Bolwell MA, DPhil

Faculty Co-ordinator,
In-service Activities, Brighton Polytechnic

Charles Letts & Co Ltd
London, Edinburgh & New York

First published 1986
by Charles Letts & Co Ltd
Diary House, Borough Road, London SE1 1DW

Illustrations: Edward Ripley, Sally Michel, Brian Stimpson,
Alex Murphy

ISBN 0 85097 661 8

Printed in Great Britain by
Charles Letts (Scotland) Ltd

Acknowledgements

The authors and publishers are grateful to the
following for permission to reproduce
photographs and extracts in this book:
Aerofilms Ltd. p 20 Fig. 5.2, p 21 Fig. 5.3, p 60
Fig. 21.2, p 97 Fig. 38.1, p 100 Fig. 39.1, p 114
Fig. 44.1, p 120 Fig. 46.3; The J. Allan Cash
Photolibrary p 81 Fig. 30.1(b); Barnaby's Picture
Library p 57 Fig. 20.1, p 80 Fig. 30.1(a), p 101
Fig. 39.2, p 103 Fig. 40.1; British Airports
Authority 1981 p 32 Fig. 9.3; Camera Press Ltd.
p 28 Fig. 8.1, p 31 Fig. 9.1(a), p 36 Fig. 11.2, p 37
Fig. 11.4(a), p 40 Fig. 13.2, p 65 Fig. 24.2, p 73
Fig. 27.1, p 106 Fig. 41.4, p 121 Fig. 47.1; Citroën
Cars Ltd. p 118 Fig. 46.1; James Davis
Photography p 43 Fig. 14.2, p 48 Fig. 16.2, p 51
Fig. 17.2, p 55 Fig. 19.2; French Government
Tourist Office p 14 Fig. 2.2; Bruno Vignol/French
Railways Ltd. p 89 Fig. 34.1; Freytag-Berndt &
Artaria KG, Vienna p 82 Fig. 31.1; German
National Tourist Office p 79 Figs. 29.3(b), (c), (d);
German Press Agency, Hamburg p 79
Fig. 29.3(a); Institut Géographique National,
Paris p 13 Fig. 2.1; Italian State Tourist Office
(E.N.I.T), London p 86 Fig. 33.1; p 92 Fig. 35.2,
p 116 Fig. 45.1; Manchester Guardian & Evening
News plc p 74 Fig. 27.2; Novosti Press Agency
p 45 Fig. 15.2, p 61 Fig. 22.1; Olympic Holidays
Ltd. p 31 Fig. 9.1(b); Royal Ministry of Foreign
Affairs, Norway p 54 Fig. 18.2; Scandinavian
Airlines System p 93 Fig. 36.1; Times
Newspapers Ltd. p 117 Fig. 45.4; Wayland
Picture Library p 57 Fig. 20.2

Preface

This series of books has been written to help you to do well in geography and enjoy the subject both in and out of school. In the past much geography teaching was concerned with facts, and pupils were expected to learn by heart as much information as possible.

Examinations were made up of questions which tested this knowledge and those with a good memory could score high marks. In recent years there has been a change of emphasis and now geography lessons are not solely a means of providing information. Facts are still important, but geography is also concerned with ideas and concepts, and to be good at the subject you must understand these and also master the skills which are used by geographers.

Some facts, such as population statistics, are soon out-of-date, whereas ideas which help to explain population change and movement are always important when we are trying to understand the world in which we live. These ideas can only be fully appreciated if we also understand the maps and charts which are used to explain them. To succeed in geography you must know, and be able to use, the skills associated with the subject. Some of these skills, such as the plotting of information on maps and the interpretation of aerial photographs of the landscape, are distinctive to geography. Other skills, for example calculating and classifying, are shared with other subjects such as biology and mathematics. Because it is impossible to know all the facts, it is also especially important that you have the skills which will help you to find out information from atlases and reference books.

In this book there is a systematically planned development of the ideas and skills you will need to give you a sound groundwork in geography. These ideas and skills have been included in a series of carefully selected topics which are about Europe, and which also provide up-to-date information as well as a variety of activities for you to do. These activities will develop your understanding of geographical ideas and skills and should prove to you that this subject is interesting as well as stimulating. Ideas and skills which you learn now will form a foundation for examination work in a few years' time. In this way you will be sowing the seeds for success in future examinations.

In preparing this series we have received expert advice and invaluable support from Norman Law, Head of Geography and Assistant Head of Upper School, Waingel's Copse School, near Reading. Norman's perceptive and constructive comments are based on his own extensive experience as a teacher, examiner and author. We are also grateful for the support and encouragement received from the editorial staff at Charles Letts Limited. The firm's initial research, on the needs of teachers and students of geography in the early years of secondary education, has provided the guidelines for the structure and approach used in these books.

C J Lines
L H Bolwell
February, 1986

4

Contents

Transport

Industry

Introduction

Aims

Like Book 1, this book is designed to provide the basis for one year's work in geography, given the fact that the work will be supplemented by other material including TV programmes and videotapes. It has been written for pupils of average and above average ability who have already used Book 1 and are therefore ready to build on the techniques and ideas in that book.

Many of the aims of this book are identical with those for Books 1 and 3 but there are some which are specific to the study of Europe and its problems. After working systematically through this book pupils should be:

1 equipped with a range of skills and concepts relevant to geography, some of which may also be applicable to other subjects such as English and mathematics;

2 able to appreciate systems and processes and the significance of location as a geographical concept;

3 able to observe, record and analyze simple geographical phenomena from maps, photographs, diagrams and other information;

4 able to consult maps, atlases and other reference material to find out information;

5 more aware of some of the links between Britain and the neighbouring countries of Europe, particularly the other member countries of the EEC;

6 more aware of some of the problems to be found in Europe, many of which also occur in Britain and elsewhere;

7 more knowledgeable about the physical and human geography of Europe;

8 able to study independently and, when necessary, as a member of a team;

9 able to regard geography as an interesting and relevant part of the school curriculum.

Structure

This book continues the pattern already established in Book 1. The six basic themes are examined in a European context. The themes are:

Mapwork and physical geography
Climate, weather, soils and vegetation
Agriculture
Population and settlement
Transport
Industry

Each theme consists of eight topics which are presented as self-contained units. Nevertheless, the units are related to one another and provide a progressive development of the theme. Each topic occupies two pages, with information on the left-hand page and related activities on the facing page. The concepts and skills identified with each unit have been plotted on the Analysis Table on pages 8 and 9.

Where appropriate, answers to the activities have been provided at the end of the book, together with a glossary of terms used. There is a contents list, containing details of each unit on pages 4 and 5, which can be used as an index.

There are no fieldwork activities included in this book as there are likely to be few, if any, opportunities for first-hand observations in Europe.

Geography has an important rôle to play in creating an awareness of environmental problems and issues. A number of case studies have been included which demonstrate the nature of specific problems, such as traffic congestion in Brussels, and the solutions which have been introduced to deal with them.

Concepts and skills

There has been a trend in recent years to pay particular attention in schools to the teaching of concepts and skills. This trend is linked to concern about educational standards, questioning about what is being taught and the need to agree certain standards and levels of achievement which should be reached during the years of compulsory education. As a result of research in the last decade by the Schools' Council, the Geographical Association, Her Majesty's Inspectorate and numerous other organizations and teachers' groups, it is possible to draw up a list of geographical concepts and skills. Moreover, a consensus is beginning to emerge as to what concepts and skills should have been acquired during the first three years of secondary schooling. These years are crucial since many pupils abandon geography at the end of the third year when alternative options can be selected. They are also vital years because sound practice now will provide the background for examination success, in the GCSE, later. The choice of concepts and skills in the Analysis Table is based on an extensive study of the various suggestions which have been put forward. The concepts covered in this book are wide-ranging and include relief on maps, core industrial areas and environmental pollution. The concepts are reinforced by structured exercises, questions and other activities.

There are four main groups of skills used by geographers and a wide range of examples of these are used in this book. They are geographical skills, numeracy and graphicacy, writing and speaking skills, and study skills. Geographical skills give the subject its distinctiveness as a discipline and include the plotting and analysis of spatial patterns. Numeracy skills are shared with other disciplines as are some of the skills concerned with graphicacy, such as the drawing of graphs. Other graphical skills, including the drawing of field sketches and the interpretation of statistical data, are more closely related to geography.

The third group of skills cannot be ignored by geographers since they are concerned with such things as writing clear accounts, describing processes and being able to present coherent arguments.

The final group of skills are study skills. These involve pupils in searching out information from reference books and studying atlases and other forms of evidence. There are many opportunities in the 'Activities' pages for pupils to practise these skills and become proficient in them.

How to use this book

This book, like Books 1 and 3, has been planned so that it can be worked through systematically. Most of the information and activities are on facing pages and the units are self-contained. Each book can be used as a class text, supplemented by additional material when necessary. Alternatively it can be used for private study at home or to reinforce work of a similar nature which is being taught as part of the year's geography programme.

For students working on their own it is best to read a unit, complete the exercises and then check the answers which can be found at the back of the book. Questions which have not been answered correctly should be reviewed and repeated. If the work is being revised for a test it is worthwhile to get someone else to ask questions on the units which have been learned. This form of assessment is best done orally.

Analysis of Concepts and Skills
SKILLS

	Topic Units	Analysing, questioning	Calculating	Classifying	Constructing charts and questionnaires	Correlating	Decision making	Discussing	Interpreting	Investigating	Making maps	Measuring	Presenting relevant arguments
	MAPWORK AND PHYSICAL GEOGRAPHY												
1	The map of Europe	●	●	●							●	●	
2	Map symbols		●						●				
3	Contours		●								●	●	
4	Cross-sections		●		●						●		
5	Photographs	●						●	●				
6	Latitude and longitude		●									●	
7	Mountain building								●				
8	Volcanoes								●				●
	CLIMATE, WEATHER, SOILS AND VEGETATION												
9	Climate and weather	●	●				●					●	●
10	The water cycle					●	●		●	●			●
11	Pressure and winds	●				●			●				
12	Ocean currents								●				
13	The tundra lands of the north	●							●				●
14	The coniferous forest lands					●			●	●			
15	Continental grasslands				●				●				
16	The Mediterranean lands	●							●			●	●
	AGRICULTURE												
17	Farming in Europe	●	●	●	●	●			●				
18	Farming the marginal lands	●							●				
19	Mediterranean fruit farming								●				●
20	Grain cultivation	●			●	●			●				●
21	Land reclamation	●		●					●	●			
22	Farming in Eastern Europe								●				●
23	Dairy farming in Denmark	●				●			●	●			
24	The Common Agricultural Policy						●						●
	POPULATION AND SETTLEMENT												
25	The population of Western Europe		●		●	●			●				
26	Movements of people inside countries				●	●			●				
27	Immigration			●	●				●				●
28	Rural depopulation						●		●		●		●
29	The functional regions of a city	●							●				●
30	Decay and redevelopment				●				●				●
31	The Central Business District	●			●				●				●
32	A hierarchy of towns			●	●	●			●				
	TRANSPORT												
33	Road networks		●		●								
34	Rail networks		●		●				●				
35	Airports		●	●	●			●			●		●
36	Air networks	●	●						●			●	
37	Inland waterways	●					●		●		●		●
38	Coastal ports	●	●				●		●		●		●
39	Transport in cities	●	●			●			●				●
40	Transport – suitability and costs	●	●				●		●		●		●
	INDUSTRY												
41	Mining	●	●			●	●	●	●				●
42	Iron and steel		●				●		●				●
43	Oil refining	●	●				●						●
44	Industrial concentration				●				●				●
45	Industrial trends	●									●		●
46	Governments and industrial location	●	●			●	●	●	●				●
47	The tourist industry	●							●		●		●
48	Problems of tourism				●		●	●					●

CONCEPTS

Using an atlas	Using reference books	Writing descriptions	Accessibility	Change	Conflict	Costs	Density	Development	Direction	Distance	Distribution	Height	Location	Movement	Networks	Quality	Symbols	Systems	Time	
			•	•				•			•									1
•									•	•		•	•				•			2
												•					•			3
									•			•								4
•		•											•							5
									•	•	•		•							6
											•		•	•					•	7
	•	•											•							8
											•									9
•														•				•		10
									•		•			•						11
•		•							•		•			•						12
		•									•		•							13
	•	•	•	•				•			•		•							14
		•								•	•		•							15
		•									•		•			•				16
											•		•							17
		•											•	•						18
				•							•		•							19
											•		•							20
				•				•											•	21
								•												22
				•				•												23
								•												24
		•					•													25
•			•	•					•					•		•				26
				•										•						27
				•									•	•						28
		•									•		•							29
				•				•												30
			•					•			•		•							31
											•									32
•			•					•		•			•	•	•	•	•			33
			•		•					•				•	•				•	34
•			•				•			•	•		•	•						35
	•					•	•							•	•				•	36
•				•		•	•								•				•	37
			•	•				•			•		•							38
•			•	•			•	•						•						39
			•			•				•	•					•				40
			•			•					•		•						•	41
			•	•		•					•		•							42
•			•			•				•	•		•	•	•					43
			•	•	•						•		•	•					•	44
				•	•		•	•			•		•			•				45
				•	•	•	•	•					•	•		•				46
	•		•	•						•			•			•				47
			•	•	•	•		•								•				48

Mapwork and physical geography

Unit 1

The map of Europe

1.1 Britain in Europe

If it were not for the 33 kilometres of the English Channel which separate Britain from France, these islands would be part of mainland Europe. In the past Britain developed an overseas empire which gave us closer ties with distant parts of the world such as Australia, than with neighbouring countries in Europe.

In recent years, however, Britain's links with other parts of the world have weakened and our connections with Western Europe have become stronger. Improved communications have helped to bring Britain closer to Europe. Many people living in south-east England often take the boat or hovercraft to one of the French ports to do a day's shopping. Many towns in Britain are crowded with young people during the summer months. They have come from different parts of Europe to learn English and study our way of life. Football and other sports teams travel to fixtures in European cities and people whose parents went no further than Blackpool for their holidays are regular visitors to Torremolinos and other Mediterranean resorts. Western Europe is also

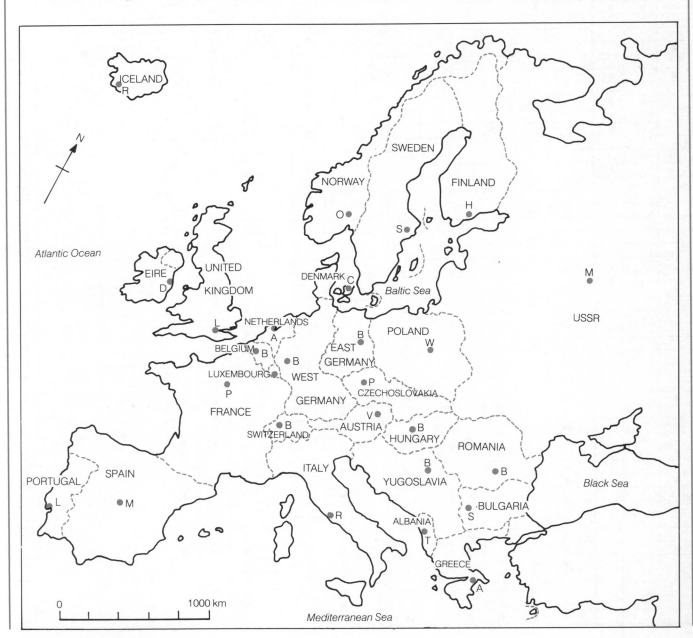

Fig. 1.1 Britain in Europe

the largest market for British goods and in return we buy European cars, food, household goods and clothing. An understanding of the geography of Europe, particularly Western Europe, is therefore next in importance to a study of Britain.

The units in this book will help you to understand our neighbours in Europe and also introduce you to new geographical techniques and ideas.

1.2 European groupings

Many of the countries of Europe have grouped themselves into a number of organizations. Some of these, such as the Warsaw Treaty Organization, are concerned with defence, while others, such as the EEC (European Economic Community), aim at economic, social and political unity. There are clear political differences between Eastern and Western Europe and since Britain is closely identified with Western Europe,

particularly the EEC countries, this book will focus, in the main, on the western half of the continent.

Activities

A Look at Fig. 1.1 opposite which shows the countries of Europe and the first letters of the names of their capital cities.

Using an atlas, make a list of the countries and write beside each one the name of the capital city.

B The three main trade groupings in Europe are the countries belonging to: the EEC; COMECON (Council for Mutual Economic Assistance); and EFTA (European Free Trade Association).

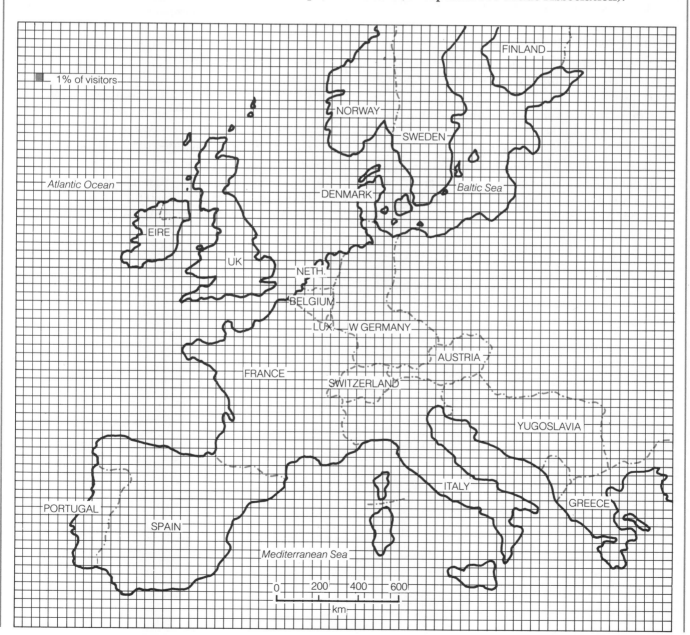

Fig. 1.2 Holiday visitors from the United Kingdom

Activities continued

At the present time the membership of these associations is:

EEC – Belgium, Denmark, Eire, France, Greece, Italy, Luxembourg, Netherlands, Portugal, Spain, UK, West Germany.

COMECON – Bulgaria, Czechoslovakia, East Germany, Hungary, Poland, Romania, USSR.

EFTA – Austria, Finland (part member), Iceland, Norway, Sweden, Switzerland.

(a) Make a copy of the outline of Europe and the political boundaries from Fig. 1.1.

(b) Shade in blue the members of the EEC.

(c) Shade in red the members of COMECON.

(d) Shade in green the members of EFTA.

(e) Choose another colour for the countries which do not belong to any of the three trade groupings.

(f) Add a key to your map.

C Make another copy of the outline of Europe and mark on the capital cities but not the political boundaries.

The approximate flying times from London: to Paris is 1 hour; to Oslo 2 hours; to Helsinki 3 hours; and to Moscow 4 hours.

(a) With London as the centre use a pair of compasses to make circles and semi-circles for the 1 hour, 2 hours, 3 hours and 4 hours flying times from London.

(b) How many European capitals are within approximately 1 hour's flying time from London?

(c) Name the countries that are between 1 and 2 hours' flying time from London.

(d) What is the approximate flying time to Rome?

D The table below shows which countries British people visit in Europe for their holidays.

Country	%	Country	%
Austria	3	Netherlands	5
Belgium/Lux.	4	Norway/Sweden/Fin.	2
Denmark	1	Portugal	3
France	31	Spain	21
Greece	6	Switzerland	3
Italy	7	Yugoslavia	2
		Others	4

Table 1.1

(a) Make a tracing of Fig. 1.2. Show the percentage of British people visiting each country by colouring in the correct number of squares. Put the 'Others' percentage under the key.

(b) What is the name of the British territory in Europe which is included in the 'Others' percentage?

(c) What percentage of British people go on holiday to countries which have a coastline on the Mediterranean or Adriatic Seas?

Unit 2

Map symbols

2.1 A French map

Fig. 2.1 below is part of a French map showing the valley of the River Loire at Sully-sur-Loire. Just to the north of this extract is the forest of Orléans.

The French equivalent of the British Ordnance Survey is the Institut Géographique National which publishes detailed maps of France at different scales. The scale of this map is

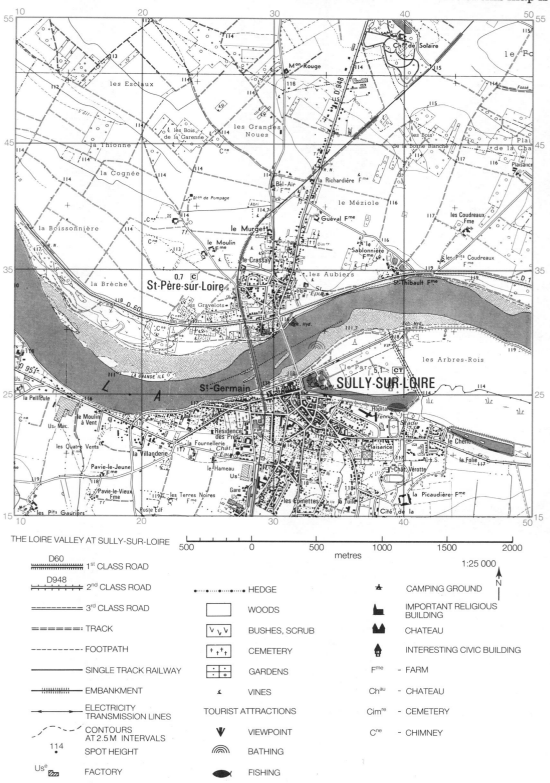

THE LOIRE VALLEY AT SULLY-SUR-LOIRE

1:25 000

D60 ══════	1ST CLASS ROAD
D948 ══════	2nd CLASS ROAD
══════	3rd CLASS ROAD
══════	TRACK
--------	FOOTPATH
────────	SINGLE TRACK RAILWAY
╫╫╫╫╫	EMBANKMENT
←───→	ELECTRICITY TRANSMISSION LINES
∿∿	CONTOURS AT 2.5M INTERVALS
114	SPOT HEIGHT
Us^e ▱	FACTORY

•·•·•·•·	HEDGE
▭	WOODS
v v v	BUSHES, SCRUB
+ + +	CEMETERY
⬚	GARDENS
↯	VINES

TOURIST ATTRACTIONS

⩔	VIEWPOINT
◉	BATHING
🐟	FISHING

⛺	CAMPING GROUND
▮	IMPORTANT RELIGIOUS BUILDING
⏏	CHATEAU
♠	INTERESTING CIVIC BUILDING
F^me	- FARM
Ch^au	- CHATEAU
Cim^re	- CEMETERY
C^ne	- CHIMNEY

Fig. 2.1 The Loire Valley at Sully-sur-Loire

Fig. 2.2
The château at
Sully-sur-Loire

1:25 000. This means that 1 centimetre on the map equals 25 000 centimetres or 250 metres on the ground. The Ordnance Survey publishes maps on the same scale in Britain.

This French map contains a great deal of detail about routeways, land use and landforms. In addition it gives information which is of value to tourists.

Many visitors come to this region of France which is famous for its large country houses, called châteaux, many of which are open to the public. A grid has been added to the map to help locate places.

Activities

A Use an atlas to answer these questions.

(a) In which direction is the River Loire flowing?
(b) In which highland region does the River Loire rise?
(c) Which direction is Paris from Sully-sur-Loire?
(d) How far in a straight line is Orléans from Sully?
(e) What is the name of the large port at the head of the Loire estuary?

B 1 What are the meanings of the symbols at:

(a) 309453; **(b)** 303454;
(c) 207357; **(d)** 407458;
(e) 303352; **(f)** 402250;
(g) 206453; **(h)** 201352;
(i) 104159?

B 2 Give six-figure map references for the following places:

(a) the château at Sully-sur-Loire;
(b) a bathing area;
(c) an interesting civic building;
(d) a camping site;
(e) a viewpoint;
(f) an important religious building;
(g) Plaisance Farm (4035);
(h) the cemetery (2015).

C Use the nearest spot height or contour to give the height of the following places:

(a) La Sablonnière Farm (3035);
(b) La Richardière Farm (3035);
(c) The factory (1015);
(d) Les bois de la Garenne (2045);
(e) the viewpoint.

D How far is it to the nearest 100 metres in a straight line from the viewpoint (3025) to:

(a) the interesting civic building;
(b) the Château Vérotte (309154);
(c) the centre of La Grande Ile?

E **(a)** Which covers more of the map area, woods or vines?
(b) Which is the larger settlement, St Père-sur-Loire or Sully-sur-Loire?
(c) What do you think the oval shapes in 3015 are likely to be?

F Design a tourist brochure for Sully-sur-Loire. Give your brochure an illustrated cover; include a sketch map to show where the important tourist places are and write a general description of the town from the evidence on the map.

Unit 3

Contours

3.1 Introduction

On the French 1:25 000 map you studied in Unit 2 there was a line symbol which represented contours. Contours are used on many maps to show the height of the land.

3.2 Drawing contour lines

Maps show parts of the earth's surface, but because they are printed on flat sheets of paper they can only show height by using symbols and figures. Height is measured as the vertical distance above the average (mean) sea level. Contour lines are the most common way of showing height on a map. They are lines which join all points of the same height above sea level.

Fig. 3.1(a) is a sketch of an island with two peaks. If the sea level rose by 100 metres the lower part of the island would disappear under the sea and the sea level would rise to line A – A. Further rises in sea level at intervals of 100 metres would result in the sea level reaching B – B, C – C, D – D and eventually E – E.

Fig. 3.1(b) shows a map of the island. The part which cannot be seen on the sketch in Fig. 3.1(a) is shown with dotted lines and shading. The imaginary increases in the height of sea level are shown as contour lines. For example, all points along line A – A are 100 metres above the existing sea level. The contours have been drawn at 100 metre intervals. In other words the vertical interval is 100 metres.

3.3 Other ways of showing height

The simplest way of showing height on a map is by drawing a dot and putting its height above sea level alongside. This is called a spot height and on the map (Fig. 3.1(b)) this method has been used to show the height of the lower peak.

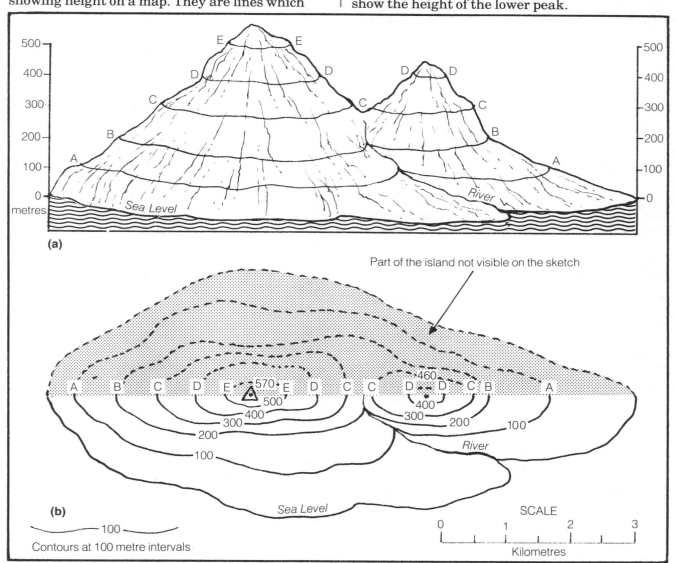

Fig. 3.1 Drawing contours

Activities

A Answer the following questions about Figs. 3.1(a) and (b).

(a) What is the height of the lower peak?

(b) What is the difference in height between the two peaks?

(c) How much would the sea have to rise before the island would disappear under the sea?

(d) What shape do the contour lines form in a river valley?

(b) Mark with an X one other place between A and B where the boat could put the tourists ashore.

(c) Use a piece of cotton or thin string to find the distance the boat must travel from A to B.

D Place a piece of tracing paper over Fig. 3.3 which shows an island with spot heights and has the 10 m contour line marked on it.

Draw contour lines for 20 m, 30 m and 40 m using the spot heights for guidance. For example, the contour line for 20 m will pass half way between the spot heights for 15 m and 25 m.

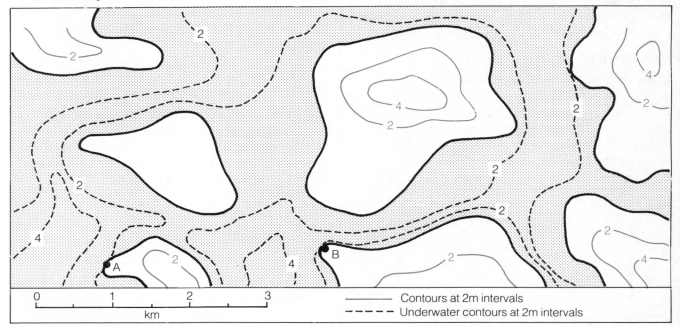

Contours at 2m intervals
Underwater contours at 2m intervals

Fig. 3.2 Some low coral islands

B **1** Make sketches using the same scale as Fig. 3.1(a) to show the shape of the land after the sea level has risen by: **(a)** 300 metres; **(b)** 500 metres.

2 Draw a map of the area after the sea level has risen by 400 metres.

C Fig. 3.2 shows a map of some low coral islands. The height of the land is shown as contours at 2 metre intervals. The depth of the sea is also shown as underwater contours at 2 metre intervals.

1 **(a)** Make a copy of the map as it would look after the sea level has risen by 2 metres. Show both land and underwater contours on your map with their correct values.

(b) Make another copy of Fig. 3.2 but do not draw on the contours above sea level.

2 A group of tourists want to get from point A to point B. The only boat available cannot sail in water that is less than 2 metres deep.

(a) Mark the course the boat must take to get from A to B.

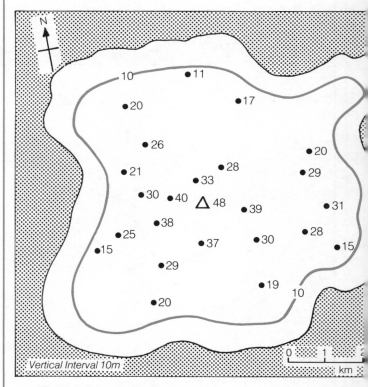

Fig. 3.3 Locating contours

Unit 4

Cross-sections

4.1 Understanding contours

At first it is not easy to imagine what the relief of the land is like from the contours on a map. Once we can 'read' contours we can recognize different types of landforms such as plateaux, low rounded hills and steep-sided valleys. To help you to understand contours you must practise drawing the landforms which they show. This is done by drawing accurate cross-sections.

4.2 Cross-sections

Cross-sections show the height of the land along a line drawn across the map.

Fig. 4.1 shows the slopes leading down to the river Marne in eastern France. The vineyards in this area are famous for their champagne. This is how to make a cross-section from A to B:

1 Place the edge of a piece of plain paper along the line of the cross-section. Mark the positions of A and B and the points where the contours touch the edge of the paper. Label each mark with the height of the contour and put a V between the marks to remind you where the land between two contours of the same height dips to form a valley. These steps are shown in Fig. 4.2

2 Choose a vertical scale for drawing the cross-section. The scale of the map is not suitable for the vertical scale because it would not show the relief clearly. Too much exaggeration must also be avoided because it would make a gently

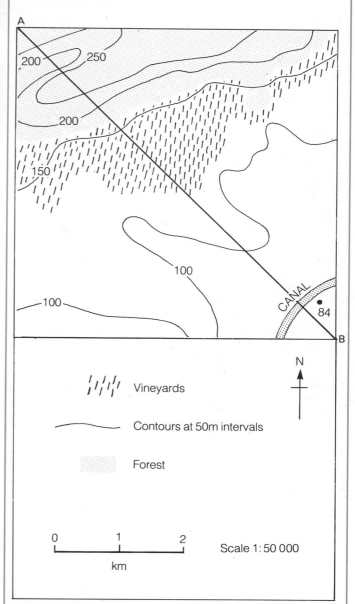

Fig. 4.1 Part of eastern France

sloping area, such as the land on the map, appear like the Alps. On this map the land is not very high and a vertical scale of 1 cm:50 m is suitable. The map itself is on a scale of 1 cm:500 m, so the vertical scale is 10 times that of the horizontal scale. We call this the **vertical exaggeration**.

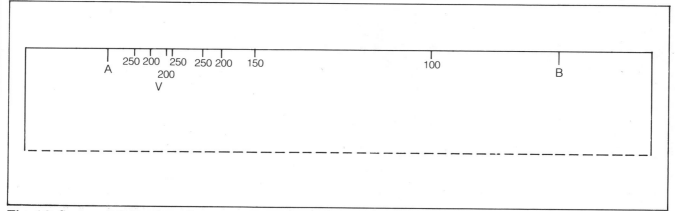

Fig. 4.2 Contour heights along the cross-section A–B in Fig. 4.1

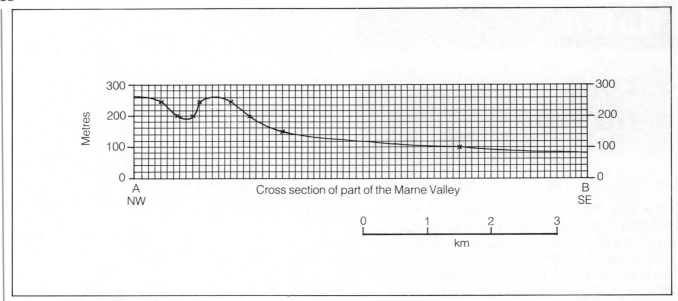

Fig. 4.3 Drawing the cross-section

3 Use graph paper for the cross-section and draw a frame marking in A and B (the same distance apart as on the map) and the vertical scale (see Fig. 4.3). Place the marked paper along the base of the frame and put dots on the graph paper at the appropriate heights. Join the dots with a smooth line, looking out for any valleys you have noted. Shade the land lightly, add the scale and a title.

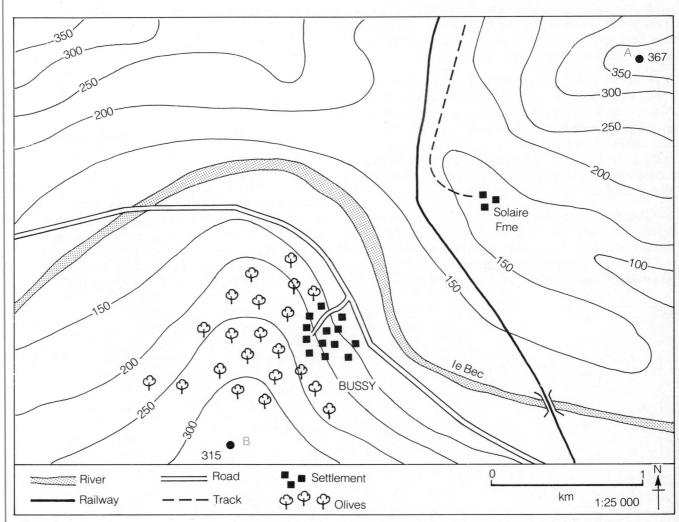

Fig. 4.4

Activities

A Use the information on pages 17 – 18 to make your own cross-section of Fig. 4.1.

B Make a cross-section of Fig. 4.4 from A to B. Give your cross-section a title.

C Draw cross-sections of maps (a), (b), (c) and (d) in Fig. 4.5 along the lines marked A – B.

D 1 Draw your own contour map of a small area in France using the key to Fig. 4.1. Your map should include two hills and a valley.

2 Make a cross-section across your map between two points marked A and B. Your cross-section should show the two hills and the valley.

E Match the cross-sections (i), (ii) and (iii) in Fig. 4.6 with the correct lines marked A – B, C – D, and E – F on the map.

Fig. 4.5

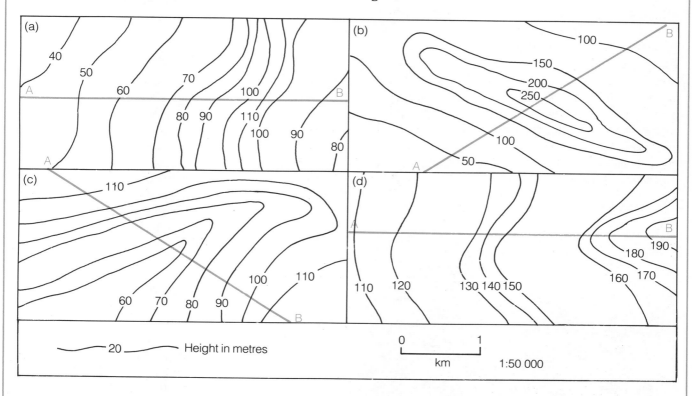

Fig. 4.6

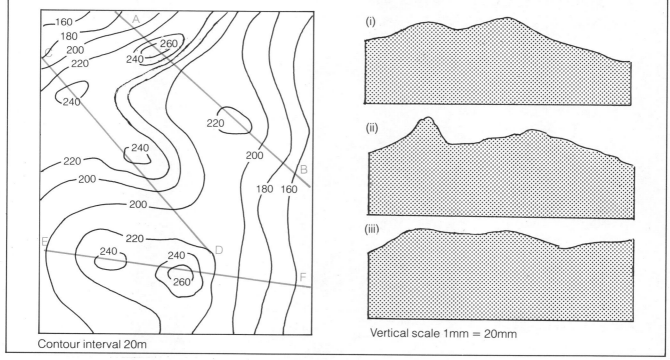

Unit 5

Photographs

5.1 Ground level photographs

Photographs play a very important part in geography. They are an accurate record of a place or scene and often contain a great deal of geographical information. The most common type of photograph you will find in books and magazines is one taken at ground level. It may be a close-up of such subjects as people, plants or buildings, or it may be a landscape view like Fig. 5.1 – a photograph of a farm in the Weiringermeer Polder in Holland.

Fig. 5.1 A farm on the Weiringermeer Polder in Holland

This flat countryside was once the sea bed. It has been drained and is now used as farmland. It is below sea level and is protected from flooding by dykes. The farms are small and usually consist of a large barn for cattle and storage, and a house for the farmer and his family. These buildings and some of the Friesian cattle can be seen in the photograph. Tall poplars and other trees have been planted around the farmstead to act as a windbreak. What the photograph cannot show is the patterns and shape of the fields, roads, drainage channels and settlements. These can best be seen on an oblique aerial photograph.

5.2 Oblique aerial photographs

This type of photograph is taken from an aircraft with the camera pointing at an angle to the ground. The view is similar to that which you get from a tall building or an aircraft window.

Fig. 5.2 is an oblique aerial photograph of the Weiringermeer Polder. It shows that the field and road system forms a grid-iron pattern (the roads and field boundaries are straight and meet at right angles), with farm houses at regular intervals. The dark stripes across some of the fields mark lines of tile drains under the ground. These carry surplus water to a network of ditches and canals. The surplus water is eventually pumped over the protecting dykes into the sea.

Oblique aerial photographs, or photographs taken from high points to show the surrounding landscape, are extremely useful. They give a view which can show small details such as houses, as well as broad patterns such as settlement distribution and land use. If an oblique aerial photograph is put beside a map of the same area, a great deal of information can be learned by geographers.

Fig. 5.2
An oblique aerial photo of the Weiringermeer Polder

Fig. 5.3 An oblique aerial photo of the Dutch coast at Noordwijk aan zee

Activities

A **(a)** Find the Weiringermeer Polder in your atlas. It is sometimes called the North-West Polder. Describe its location.

(b) Draw a sketch of the ground level photograph (Fig. 5.1), adding the following labels: road, pasture, farmhouse, barn, Friesian cattle, windbreak.

B Fig. 5.3 is an oblique aerial photograph of the Dutch coast at Noordwijk aan zee. The beach of fine sand is covered by rows of canvas shelters. Behind the beach are sand dunes and then cultivated polders.

(a) Find Noordwijk aan zee in your atlas. Which direction is it from Amsterdam?

(b) Why are canvas shelters needed?

(c) How can you tell that more than one crop is grown on the polders?

C Place a piece of tracing paper over the photograph and draw a frame. Mark in and label:

(a) the sea,

(b) beach,

(c) roads,

(d) area of dunes,

(e) a wooded area,

(f) cultivated land,

(g) a large car park,

(h) rows of shops and terraced houses,

(i) large houses in their own grounds,

(j) part of a golf course.

D **1** Write brief descriptions of:

(a) where the cars have been parked;

(b) where the people can be seen.

2 Discuss what facilities there are for tourists on this stretch of coast.

Unit 6

Latitude and longitude

6.1 Introduction

To find your position, or that of a place, accurately on a map it is necessary to have some kind of reference system. In Book 1 places on the Ordnance Survey map in Unit 2 could be located by using the National Grid. On maps of the world a similar system is used based on imaginary lines called lines of latitude and longitude.

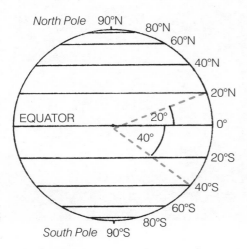

Fig. 6.1 Lines of latitude

6.2 Lines of latitude

Because the earth is almost round the starting point for lines of latitude is a line drawn round the earth at an equal distance from each pole. This line is called the Equator. Lines drawn parallel to the Equator run east–west and are called lines of latitude, or parallels. Their distance north and south of the Equator is measured from the Equator in degrees from 0° to 90° north and south as shown in Fig. 6.1.

The imaginary line running through the centre of the earth connecting the North Pole with the South Pole is called the **earth's axis**. Because the earth is tilted on its axis at an angle of 23½° there are certain important degrees of latitude. Latitudes 23½° north and 23½° south mark the points where the sun is overhead on 21st June and 21st December respectively. These

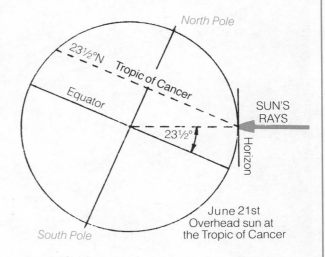

Fig. 6.2 The position of the sun on June 21st

parallels are known as the Tropics of Cancer and Capricorn.

Latitude 66½° north is the Arctic Circle and latitude 66½° south is the Antarctic Circle.

The tilt of the earth on its axis means that when the sun is overhead at the Tropic of Cancer all places between latitude 66½° north and the North Pole have 24 hours of daylight. Throughout the 24 hours the sun is always in the sky. At this time places between the South Pole and the Antarctic Circle are in darkness and the sun never appears above the horizon. On December 21st when the sun is overhead at the Tropic of Capricorn the situation is reversed. The Arctic Circle and latitudes north of it are in darkness while the Antarctic Circle and latitudes south of it have 24 hours of daylight.

6.3 Lines of longitude

Lines joining the Poles running north–south and at right angles to the parallels are called lines of longitude, or meridians. They are numbered from

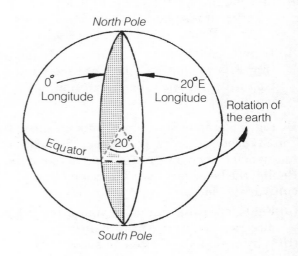

Fig. 6.3 Lines of longitude

the Greenwich **Meridian** which is called the **Prime Meridian**. From this line longitude is measured in degrees, taking angles from the earth's axis and the 0° line of longitude as shown in Fig. 6.3.

There are 180° of longitude eastwards from the Prime Meridian and 180° westwards. 180° E longitude and 180° W are the same line since there are 360° in a circle. Degrees of longitude meet at the Poles, and are furthest apart at the Equator.

Both lines of latitude and longitude are measured in degrees and minutes. For example, the City of London is located at latitude 51°. 32′ N and longitude 0°. 06′ W.

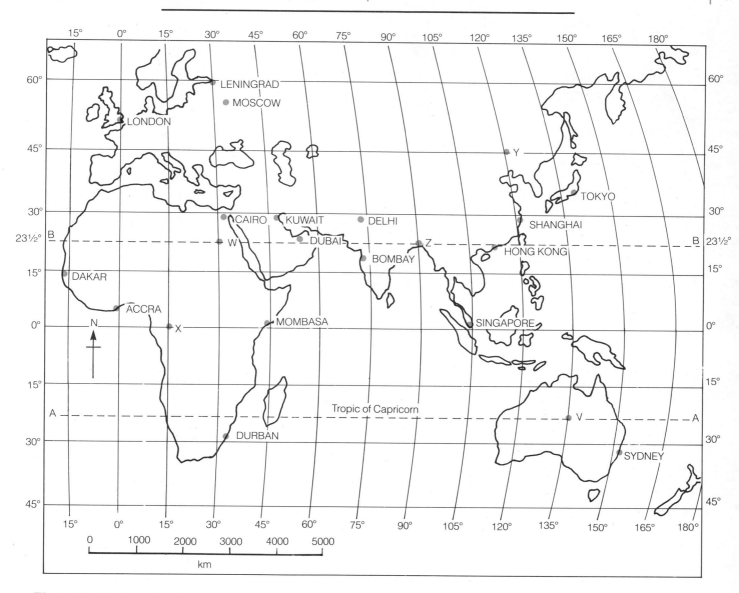

Fig. 6.4 Latitude and longitude

Activities

A Look at Fig. 6.4.

(a) What is the latitude of line A – A?

(b) What is line B – B called?

(c) What is the approximate latitude of:
  (i) Leningrad;
 (ii) Dubai;
(iii) Cairo;
(iv) Mombasa;
 (v) Durban?

(d) What is the approximate longitude of:
  (i) Cairo;
 (ii) Accra;
(iii) Shanghai;
(iv) Sydney;
 (v) Dakar?

(e) How many cities shown on the map are between the tropics?

(f) What is the line of longitude called which runs through London?

B What are the latitudes and longitudes of the places marked V, W, X, Y and Z on Fig. 6.4?

Activities continued

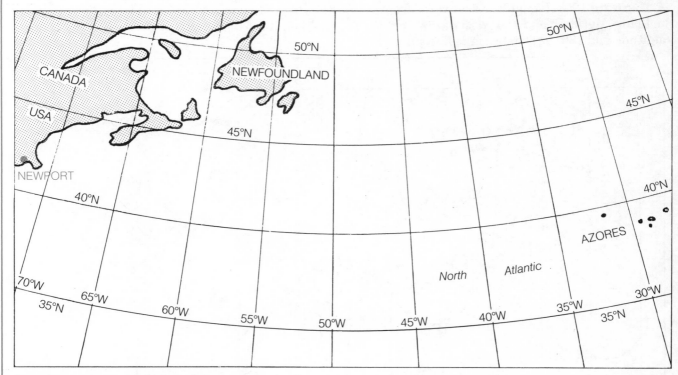

Fig. 6.5 The Trans-Atlantic Yacht Race

C Fig. 6.5 shows part of the North Atlantic between Britain and North America. During a Trans-Atlantic yacht race from Britain to Newport in the United States the yachts radioed their positions as follows (latitude is always given first):

Firefly	34°. 40′ N, 61°. 10′ W
Roger	41°. 10′ N, 36°. 03′ W
Spice II	38°. 01′ N, 41°. 00′ W
Dasher	37°. 30′ N, 68°. 10′ W
Cloud	42°. 50′ N, 68°. 02′ W
Gypsy	40°. 01′ N, 60°. 49′ W

Intrepid	44°. 00′ N, 47°. 20′ W
Emile	37°. 40′ N, 52°. 40′ W
Dragon	41°. 05′ N, 58°. 10′ W
Nancy	45°. 00′ N, 59°. 50′ W

(a) Plot the position of the ten yachts on a copy of Fig. 6.5. Put the name of the yacht beside its position.
(b) Which yacht is nearest to the finish at Newport?
(c) Which yacht is the furthest south?
(d) Which yacht is nearest to the islands of the Azores?

Unit 7

Mountain building

7.1 The earth's crust

The earth we live on has a very thin shell of rock called the crust. It is thinnest under the oceans and thickest under the continents. The hollows in the crust which are filled by the oceans are called ocean basins. The large land masses are called the continents.

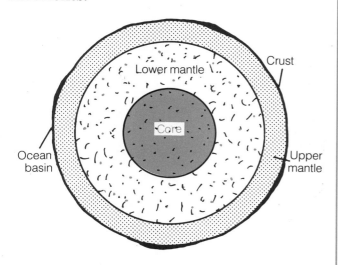

Fig. 7.1 Inside the earth

The continents are mainly made of granite whereas under the ocean basins there is a hard, dense rock called basalt. Beneath the crust is the upper mantle, a layer of solid rock which, with the crust, gives the earth a rigid shell. Lower down the rock is under great pressure and heat which makes it partially molten. This region is called the lower mantle. The centre of the earth is called the core and it is made of nickel and iron.

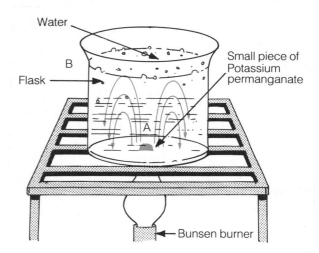

Fig. 7.3 Convection currents

7.2 Convection

When gases and liquids are heated from below they expand, become lighter and rise. This movement is called convection. At a higher level the gas or liquid may cool and spread out. It will then contract, become heavier and sink back again to its original position. This happens beneath the earth's crust. Heat from the core causes the molten rock of the lower mantle, which is like a thick syrup, to flow towards the crust. Nearer the surface it cools, spreads out and then sinks back to be heated again.

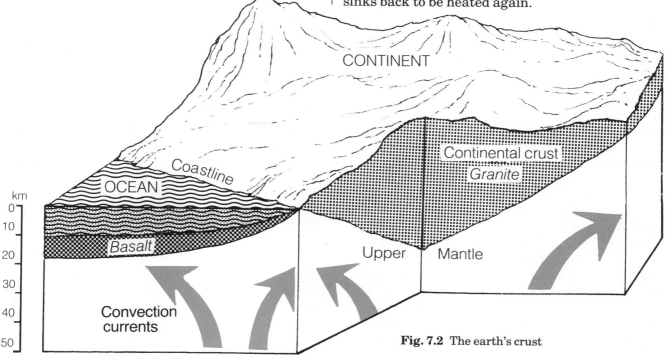

Fig. 7.2 The earth's crust

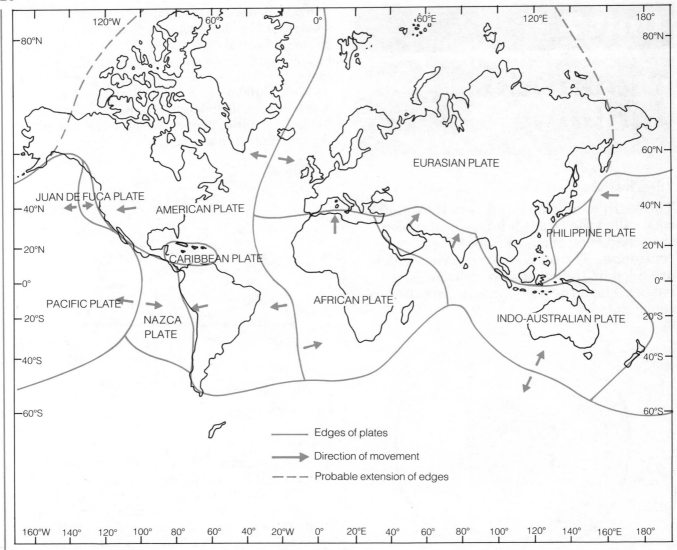

Fig. 7.4 Plates of the earth's crust

7.3 Plates

The crust is very thin when compared with the size of the earth. It is made up of several pieces and therefore resembles an egg-shell which has cracks in it. These pieces are called plates. They are shown on the map above.

The plates move slowly over the mantle in the directions shown by the arrows as a result of convection. The speed varies, for example the American and Eurasian plates are drifting apart at the rate of about 1 centimetre per year.

7.4 Building mountains

These plates have been moving throughout the earth's history and one of the results has been the ridges and mountains on the earth's surface. When two plates collide, or one rides over the other, rocks on or near the earth's surface are folded and pushed up to form mountain chains.

Some mountain regions such as the Scottish Highlands and the Ardennes in Belgium were formed many hundreds of millions of years ago. They have been worn down since that time by erosion so that only their stumps remain. The most spectacular mountain chains were formed less than 50 million years ago when the Alps, Himalayas, Rockies, Andes and the island chains of Japan and the Western Pacific were pushed up. These ranges are known as the Alpine mountain system. They are made of young rocks which were folded when the ridges were pushed up. As a result they are sometimes called fold mountains.

Activities

A Look at Fig. 7.3 which shows a flask of water being heated by a Bunsen burner. Inside the flask there is a small crystal of purple potassium permanganate which dissolves as the water is heated and stains it purple. The lines show the flow of the purple water from the dissolved crystal.

(a) Which is the hottest part of the water, A or B?

(b) Why does the purple water rise to near the surface and then sink down again?

(c) What is this process called?

(d) How does this process work inside the earth?

B Look at Figs. 7.4 and 7.5. Which two plates are responsible for the formation of the following mountain ranges?

(a) Himalayas;

(b) Southern Alps of New Zealand;

(c) Alps;

(d) Andes.

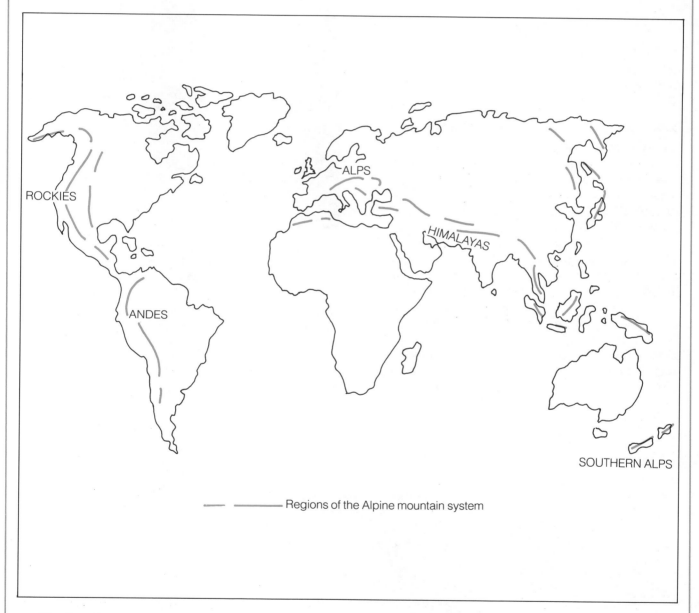

Fig. 7.5 Alpine ranges of the world

Unit 8

Volcanoes

8.1 Restless parts of the earth's crust

The edges of plates, known as plate margins, are régions where earthquakes and volcanoes occur. In Unit 7 you learned that mountain ranges of the Alpine system also occur in these regions.

Look at the plate margins on Fig. 7.4. The arrows show that at some margins the plates are moving together (converging). At other margins the plates are moving apart (diverging).

8.2 Converging and diverging plates

When plates move together a zone of folding and weakness occurs in the earth's crust. Through these weaknesses molten rock, called magma, oozes up to the surface from the mantle. At the surface if forms a volcano. From time to time pressure from below may cause a volcano to erupt.

Fig. 8.2 shows the position of Mount St Helens in the Cascade Ranges of the USA. This volcano is one of the hundreds forming a 'ring of fire' around the Pacific Ocean. In 1980 Mount St Helens erupted with tremendous force covering a huge area with volcanic ash. Pressure from below forced magma to rise inside the volcano. Hot gases caused an explosion sending a cloud of gas, dust and ash into the sky. Most of the sixty people who died were suffocated by the hot ash.

Fig. 8.1 Irazu volcano in Costa Rica erupts

Diverging plates are found mainly on the ocean beds. As they diverge the edges buckle up into a series of ridges. Material from the mantle cools between the ridges and spreads over the sea floor. Volcanoes develop close to these ridges and may build up until they form islands in mid-ocean. The island of Surtsey near Iceland was formed in this way in 1963.

Fig. 8.2 Converging plates on the USA Pacific coast

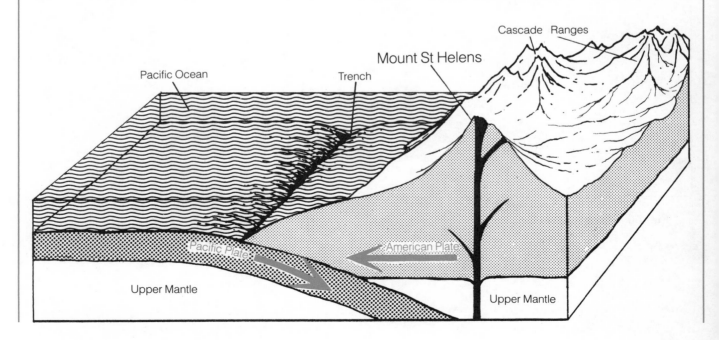

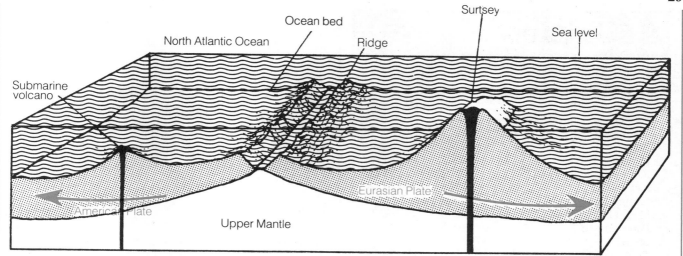

8.3 Other regions with volcanic rocks

During the long history of the earth, plates have changed their positions and molten magma which once flowed out at the plate margins may still remain, usually as outcrops of hard basalt or other hard rocks. Some magma which hardened beneath the earlier surface has now been exposed by the erosion of the rocks above.

Fig. 8.3 Diverging plates in the North Atlantic, near Iceland

Fig. 8.4 Volcanic regions of the world

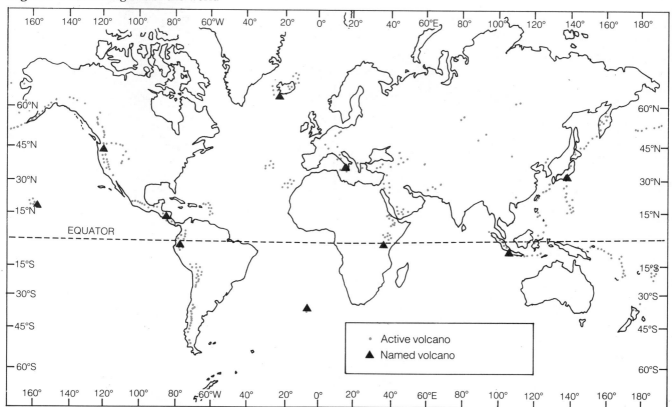

Activities

A

Volcano	Location	
Cotopaxi	0°. 30′ S	78°. 30′ W
Etna	37°. 46′ N	15°. 00′ E
Fuji-san	35°. 22′ N	138°. 44′ E
Kilimanjaro	3°. 04′ S	37°. 22′ E
Krakatoa	6°. 07′ S	105°. 24′ E
Mauna Loa	21°. 08′ N	157°. 13′ W
Mount St Helens	40°. 12′ N	122°. 11′ W
Popocatepetl	19°. 10′ N	98°. 40′ W
Surtsey	63°. 16′ N	20°. 32′ W
Tristan da Cunha	37°. 15′ S	12°. 30′ W

Table 8.1

(a) Look at Fig. 8.4 and the table above. Make a tracing of the map and mark and name on it the ten volcanoes listed in the table.

(b) Which two volcanoes in the list have been formed by divergence of plates under the Atlantic Ocean? (Look at Fig. 7.4.)

(c) Which volcano has been formed by the convergence of the African and Eurasian plates?

(d) Which volcano has been formed by convergence of the Indo-Australian and Eurasian plates?

B Write an explanation of why a new island called Surtsey appeared in the sea south of Iceland in 1963.

C Use reference books to answer the following questions about volcanoes.

(a) Which volcano destroyed Pompeii in AD 79?

(b) Which volcano exploded in AD 1883 sending clouds of dust round the world?

(c) Which volcano is considered to be sacred by the Japanese?

(d) Which volcano in the Caribbean wiped out the city of St Pierre in 1902, killing 30 000 people?

(e) Which volcano was called 'The Warrior' by the Aztecs?

D Explain why there are no active volcanoes in Britain but there are 54 in Japan.

E Look at Fig. 8.5 and describe what happened when Mount St Helens erupted in 1980.

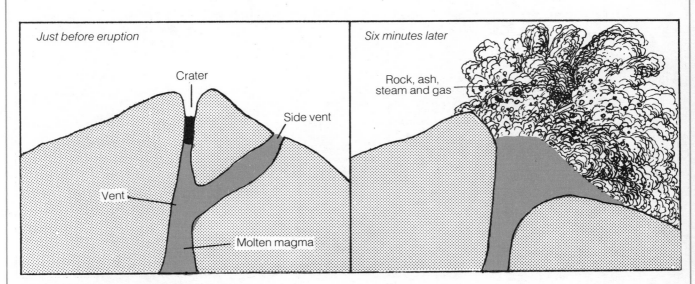

Fig. 8.5 The eruption of Mount St Helens

Climate, weather soils and vegetation

Unit 9

Climate and weather

Fig. 9.1 (b) Sunbathers in Greece

Fig. 9.1 (a) Ski-ing in the Kitzbuhel Alps

9.1 Introduction

The climates of different countries vary a great deal. Above are two typical scenes in different parts of Europe. The skiers are in Switzerland, but in winter you can see people skiing in mountain areas in many European countries.

The sunbathers are on a Greek island but again scenes like this are common in and around the Mediterranean. So what determines the climate that a country or region experiences?

9.2 Factors affecting climate

1 Latitude which, because of the tilt of the earth's axis, determines the amount of heat received from the sun. Climates generally get hotter towards the Equator.

2 The distribution of land and sea for places near the sea have a more equable climate. The sea cools down the land in summer and keeps it warm in winter.

3 Ocean currents Warm currents such as the North Atlantic Drift warm the lands which they come near. They also warm air passing over the sea towards the land. Cold currents have the opposite effect (see Unit 12).

4 Altitude Temperatures decrease with height above sea level at the approximate rate of 6.5°C for every 1000 metres. So highland areas generally have cooler climates than lowlands.

5 The location of the land related to **wind and pressure belts of the world** (see Unit 11). Britain is in the westerly wind belt all through the year so the influence of the sea is strong. The climate is characterized by mild winters, cool summers and rain all through the year. The Mediterranean lands only get the westerlies in winter. In the summer the wind belts move north with the sun. So these lands have a mild wet winter like Britain but have a hot dry summer.

9.3 Elements of climate

The main elements of the climate of any country are:

(a) temperature;
(b) the wind systems;
(c) humidity (the amount of moisture in the atmosphere);
(d) precipitation (rain, snow, hail etc).

You will read about these elements in different types of climate in Europe in the later sections of this book.

9.4 Climate and weather

Climate can be said to be the average weather. In some countries the weather patterns are generally very regular so people know what to expect. In Britain the weather is very changeable. That is why British people talk about the weather so much and why daily weather forecasts raise a great deal of interest.

To try to take into account the variations in the weather, climatic data are worked out over a long period of at least 30 years. So an average temperature of 4°C for January means that it is the average temperature for January worked out over at least 30 years.

Activities

A A weather problem

A new airport is needed. The two sites available are shown in the diagram, Fig. 9.2. The new airport must:

(a) have a main runway at least 2000 metres long and 50 metres wide;

(b) have alternative runways if possible;

(c) be located so that aircraft can land or take off into the wind.

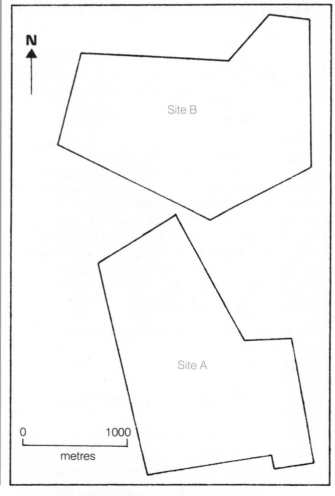

Fig. 9.2 Two possible airport locations

Fig. 9.3 Bad weather closes an airport

Two other factors affecting the choice are:

(d) strong cross winds and gales are dangerous;

(e) the airport may be closed by ice, snow, fog or low cloud. Tables 9.1 and 9.2 show the average weather conditions for the two sites.

Wind direction	Site A	Site B
N	15	36
NE	9	19
E	18	28
SE	16	11
S	41	23
SW	163	92
W	83	73
NW	20	91

Table 9.1 The number of days per year with winds from given directions

Weather conditions	Site A	Site B
low cloud	58	63
fog	18	35
gales	31	21
snow	36	9
frost	95	78
no wind	20	40

Table 9.2 The average number of days with certain limiting weather conditions

(i) Which is the better choice of site for the new airport?

(ii) Write a report giving the reasons for your choice.

Unit 10

The water cycle

The figure below shows the movement of moisture and water which we call the water cycle.

The heat of the sun draws moisture from the land and sea in the form of a gas called water vapour. This evaporation is accompanied by moisture given off by plants – the process of transpiration. In plants the moisture moves upwards from the roots to the leaves. From the surface of the leaves the moisture passes into the atmosphere. So moisture is fed into the air from both land and sea.

When moisture is forced to rise, for example when it is in a wind as it blows up over land, condensation occurs and clouds are formed. This results in precipitation in the form of rain, mist, fog, hail or snow.

Some of the precipitation runs off the surface of the land in streams and rivers. Some sinks into the ground. It then either flows through the ground to the sea or collects as ground water. As the level of the ground water builds up it may come to the surface again in springs. When the water reaches the sea it acts as a huge storage area from which the process begins again.

10.1 Moisture in the air

Warm air is able to hold more moisture than cold air. When air contains as much moisture as it can hold it is said to be **saturated**. Saturated air is said to have a **relative humidity** of 100%. If air at a certain temperature holds half of the water vapour it is able to carry the relative humidity is 50%. Relative humidity is a measure which helps us work out what the weather will be like.

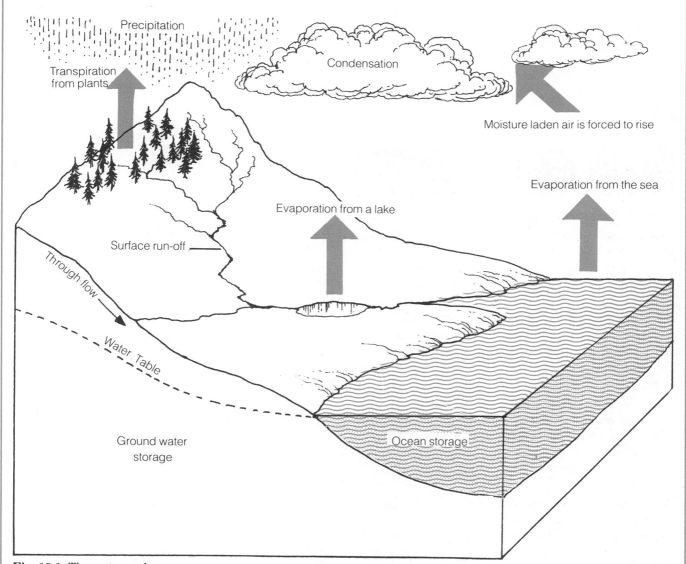

Fig. 10.1 The water cycle

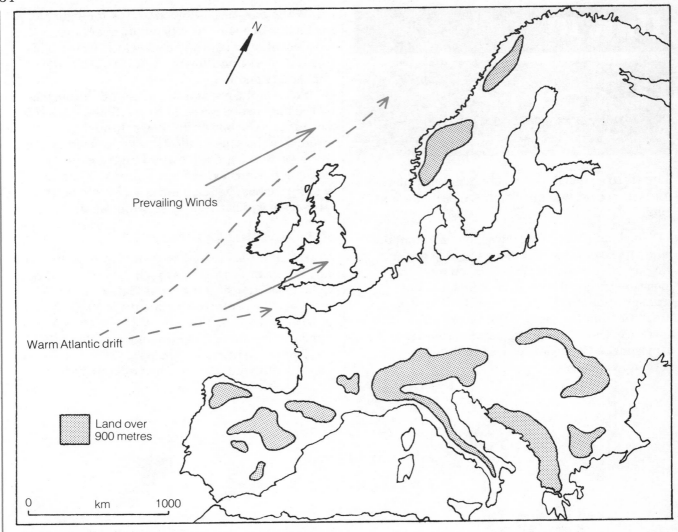

Fig. 10.2 A relief map of Europe

Activities

A Fig. 10.2 shows the highest land areas of Europe and the prevailing south-westerly winds experienced in the northern lands.

(a) Copy the map into your notebook or file.
(b) Mark on your map the chief ocean storage area.
(c) Mark 'P' on an area of north-western Europe which you think has heavy precipitation.
(d) Explain why you think 'P' is an area of heavy precipitation.
(e) With the aid of an atlas:
  (i) mark on and name two rivers which represent surface run-off;
 (ii) mark and name a large area of forest from which plant transpiration will occur;
(iii) mark a large lake from which evaporation occurs.
(f) From what direction do the prevailing winds blow in north-western Europe?
(g) Are these prevailing winds likely to have a warming influence? Give reasons for your answer.

B Fig. 10.3 is a simple model of the water cycle. Study Fig. 10.1 again.

In place of the letters in Fig. 10.1 write a word which describes each stage or process in the water cycle.

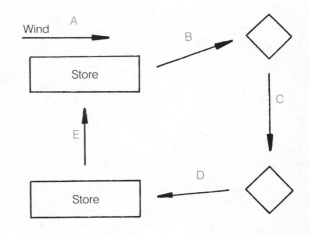

Fig. 10.3 A systems diagram of the water cycle

Unit 11

Pressure and winds

11.1 Pressure

Air has weight. The weight of the air (atmosphere) exerts pressure on the surface of the earth. This pressure is known as **atmospheric pressure**. It is measured by a mercury barometer and is expressed in millibars (mb). The average atmospheric pressure at sea level is 1013.25 mb.

Pressure varies for many reasons over the surface of the earth. Warm air expands and may become lighter than the surrounding air. This explains why there is low pressure at the Equator. The cold, heavy air at the poles forms regions of high pressure.

Difference in pressure is shown on a map by lines called **isobars**. Isobars join together places with the same atmospheric pressure.

11.2 Wind

Wind is moving air. Air flows from areas of high pressure to areas of low pressure. When pressure changes markedly over a short distance there is said to be a steep **pressure gradient**. When the gradient is steep the isobars on a map are close together. In this situation winds are strong and there may be gales. If the pressure gradient is gentle the isobars are wide apart on a map and winds are light.

11.3 Wind and pressure belts

The broad pattern of wind and pressure belts is shown in Fig. 11.1.

You can see that the winds do not blow directly from the high pressure regions to the low pressure areas. This is because the earth rotates (spins) on its axis. The spinning deflects the winds to the right in the northern hemisphere and to the left in the southern hemisphere.

As the sun moves overhead from the Tropic of Cancer in June to the Tropic of Capricorn in September the pressure and wind belts move with it (Fig. 11.3).

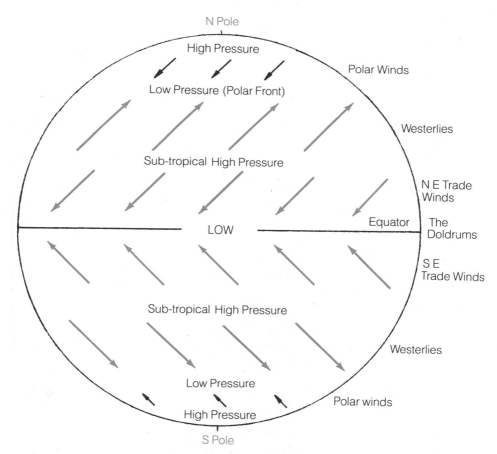

Fig. 11.1 A simple pattern of the wind and pressure belts of the world

36

Fig. 11.2 Strong winds at sea

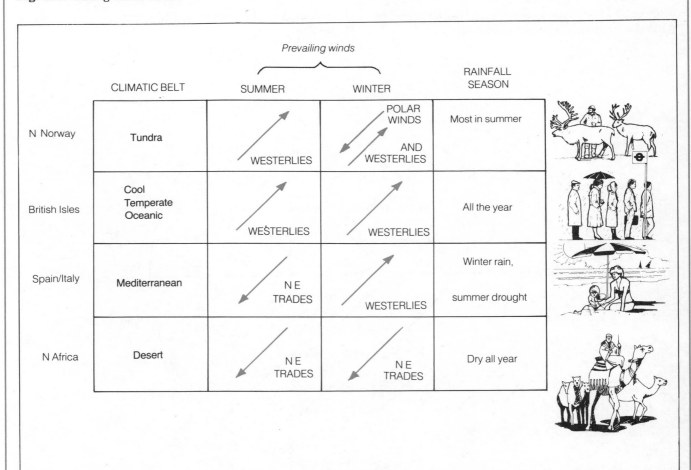

| | CLIMATIC BELT | Prevailing winds | | RAINFALL SEASON |
		SUMMER	WINTER	
N Norway	Tundra	WESTERLIES	POLAR WINDS AND WESTERLIES	Most in summer
British Isles	Cool Temperate Oceanic	WESTERLIES	WESTERLIES	All the year
Spain/Italy	Mediterranean	N E TRADES	WESTERLIES	Winter rain, summer drought
N Africa	Desert	N E TRADES	N E TRADES	Dry all year

Fig. 11.3 The effects of the seasonal shift of wind belts on the west coast of Europe and the Mediterranean

Fig. 11.4 Part of the route of *Gypsy Moth IV*

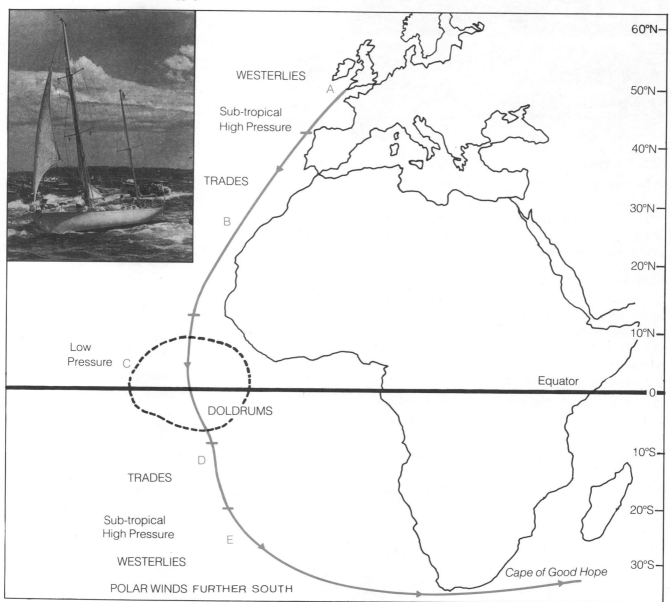

Activities

A Fig. 11.3 shows shifts in the chief wind belts on the west coast of Europe and the north-western tip of Africa. Study the table and answer these questions.

(a) Which of the winds shown are winds which blow from warm ocean areas to cooler lands?

(b) How does this table help you explain why the people of the tundra get most of their precipitation in summer?

(c) Why are the Mediterranean lands a good place climatically to spend your summer holidays?

(d) How can you tell that the NE Trade winds carry little moisture?

(e) Why does Britain get rain all through the year?

B Fig. 11.4 shows part of the route Sir Francis Chichester took with *Gipsy Moth IV* when he sailed around the world.

The route has been divided into sections each of which is shown by a letter. Figs. 11.1 and 11.3 will help you answer these questions.

(a) On section A of the route did he sail with or against the prevailing winds?

(b) What were the prevailing winds on section B? Did they help him sail south?

(c) What do we mean when we say someone is 'in the doldrums'?

(d) Why did sailors on sailing ships dislike sailing through the doldrums?

(e) What winds helped him sail around the Cape of Good Hope?

(f) Why did Sir Francis Chichester not wish to sail too far south of the Cape of Good Hope?

Unit 12

Ocean currents

12.1 Currents

When water flows in a set direction for the whole or part of a year it is known as a current. Currents which carry masses of water from one part of an ocean to another are called **ocean currents**.

12.2 Causes of ocean currents

1 Prevailing winds which blow regularly in one main direction – for example, NW Europe experiences westerly winds all the year round and the North Atlantic Drift ocean current flows in a parallel direction south-west to north-east across the Atlantic (look back at Fig. 10.2).

2 The shape of a land mass – for example the cold Labrador Current is funnelled southwards between Greenland and North America.

3 The rotation of the earth – the spinning of the earth results in currents in the North Atlantic flowing in a clockwise direction while those in the South Atlantic flow anti-clockwise.

4 Temperature differences and convection – in the enclosed Mediterranean Sea high summer temperatures cause evaporation. The water in the Mediterranean is denser and saltier than the water in the Atlantic Ocean. So, water from the Mediterranean flows along the sea bed into the Atlantic through the Strait of Gibraltar. This causes a surface current to flow into the Mediterranean from the Atlantic (Fig. 12.1).

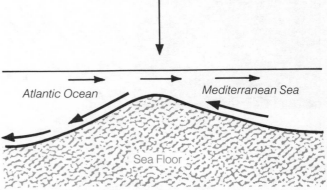

Fig. 12.1 Sea water movements at the Strait of Gibraltar

12.3 Warm and cold currents

Currents are known as warm or cold according to how they compare with surrounding water.

The North Atlantic Drift is a warm current because the water which reaches northern Europe is warmer than the sea into which it flows. In general, a current moving towards the Equator is cold; a current moving towards the Pole is warm. Check this on Fig. 12.2 to see if it is always true.

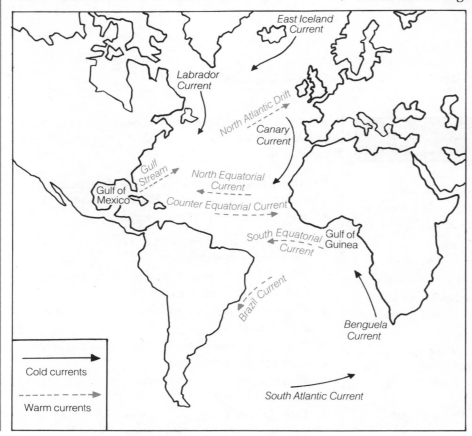

Fig. 12.2 Ocean currents in the Atlantic Ocean

Fig. 12.3 Winter in the North Atlantic

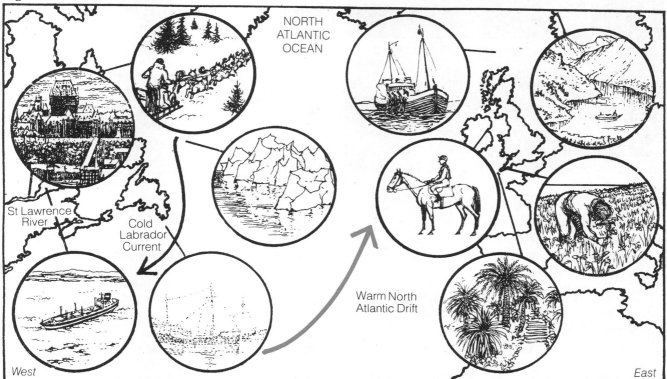

12.4 Effects of ocean currents

Ocean currents have a great effect on the climates of islands and countries they flow past.

The North Atlantic Drift helps keep British winters mild. The cold Labrador Current on the opposite side of the Atlantic cools the east coast of North America and helps cause fogs around Newfoundland.

Activities

A Study Fig. 12.2.

(a) Which two currents carry icebergs from the Arctic region into the Atlantic Ocean?

(b) From which gulf does the Gulf Stream get its name?

(c) Which current in the Atlantic Ocean gets its name from some islands it passes?

(d) Which currents cool the coastlands of south-west Africa?

B Table 12.1 shows the average temperatures for the coldest month of the year at six weather stations located on the edges of the Atlantic Ocean.

1 (a) Which station has the coldest month?
(b) Is it the one nearest the Arctic Circle?

2 Portland and Biarritz are the same distance from the Equator.
(a) Which has the lower temperature in winter?
(b) Which station is influenced by a warm ocean current?

3 (a) In general how do temperatures on the east coast of North America compare with those on the coast of Europe?
(b) From Fig. 12.2 suggest **two** reasons for this.

C Use the information in this section and the cartoon above to write an account of the effects of ocean currents upon the winter climate of coastal areas bordering the North Atlantic Ocean.

East coast of North America			*West coast of Europe*		
Place	**Approx. latitude**	**Av. temp. coldest month**	**Place**	**Approx. latitude**	**Av. temp. coldest month**
Hebron (Labrador)	58°N	−21°C	Bergen (Norway)	60.5°N	1.2°C
St John's (Newfoundland)	47.5°N	−5.5°C	Scilly Is. (England)	50°N	7.4°C
Portland (Maine)	43.5°N	−5.3°C	Biarritz (France)	43.5°N	7.8°C

Table 12.1

Unit 13

The tundra lands of the north

13.1 Location of the tundra

Near the North Pole ice desert exists. Even the warmest month has an average temperature below freezing. So plants do not grow.

Southward from the pole the temperatures rise slowly. Some plants can grow in areas where the warmest month has a temperature above freezing. Where the temperatures get warm enough for tree growth there is the great forest belt of coniferous trees. Between the ice deserts to the north and the forest to the south lie the tundra lands.

13.2 The climate of the tundra

The climate of the tundra is characterized by:

1 very long cold winters;
2 short cool summers;
3 long summer days and little daylight in midwinter;
4 little precipitation during the year;
5 most precipitation falling as snow.

In the tundra lands temperatures rise above freezing point for only two to four months in the year. Killing frosts can happen at any time of the year. Summer does not start until June but winter returns in September.

13.3 Permafrost

Permafrost is permanently frozen ground. In tundra regions the surface of the soil thaws out in summer, but just beneath the surface the ground temperature stays below freezing point all through the year. Water from melted snow and ice cannot sink into frozen ground so the surface of the land in the tundra is waterlogged during the summer months.

13.4 Vegetation in the tundra

Very few plants can live in such harsh conditions. The plants found have to complete their life cycle in the very short cool summer. Most plants are very resistant to frost and stay dormant until the weather is warmer. Most of the plants are low

Fig. 13.1

Fig. 13.2 The midnight sun over Leningrad

growing so that they are sheltered from the bitterly cold winds. The most common plants are mosses and lichens.

13.5 Living in the tundra of Norway

In northern Norway as spring begins the Lapp people move north to graze their herds of reindeer on summer pastures. They are a tough people who can live in tents made with birch poles, even when the ground is snow covered.

Many Lapps continue to wear traditional costumes and keep up their ancient beliefs and customs.

Activities

A   Opposite is a drawing of a snowmobile in the tundra in the spring.

(a) How can you tell it is still very cold?

(b) What does the snowmobile move on?

B   Study Fig. 13.3 below. It shows what different people feel about the tundra area.

(a) Why do you think young people are moving away from the tundra region?

(b) In what ways does the permafrost make mining a slow and expensive business?

(c) With the aid of an atlas explain why the army needs Arctic training.

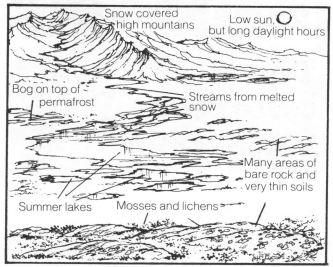

Fig. 13.4 The tundra lands in summer

(d) Name two things you have read about in this unit that attract tourists to the tundra.

(e) Make a list of the disadvantages of the tundra as a tourist region.

(f) Would you like to visit Lappland? Give reasons.

C   Fig. 13.4 is a series of sketches of part of the tundra lands in the summer.

(a) Write an account of what the sketches show.

(b) Draw a picture to show what the same region will look like in the middle of winter.

(c) Write an explanation of what your picture shows.

Fig. 13.3 Attitudes to the tundra

Unit 14

The coniferous forest lands

14.1 Introduction

A huge belt of coniferous forests extends eastwards from the mountains of Norway and the Baltic lands through to northern Siberia in Asia. These forests are found to the south of the tundra lands and north of the temperate grasslands or broad-leaved forest. The name given to this belt is the taiga and the climate which causes it is the temperate continental climate.

14.2 The climate of the taiga

The lands which experience this climate are cut off from the influence of the Atlantic Ocean. Land heats up and cools down more quickly than water. So, continental climates are characterized by a large range in temperature between summer and winter.

Winters are cold and summers are warm. The most important fact though is that the winters are long and severe. Snow covers the ground for at least half the year. Summers are short and it is during the summer that most of the rain falls, although the total amount which falls in the year is small.

14.3 Vegetation of the taiga

On the southern edges of the taiga lands coniferous trees mix with deciduous. As the climate gets harsher northwards coniferous trees such as spruce and pine predominate. Further north still the forest thins out gradually into tundra.

'Green gold'

The soils of the taiga are usually infertile. They are sandy and acid and are known as **podsols**. The trees themselves are the main source of income in taiga lands.

Eighty per cent of Finland's export trade is made up of timber products. As far as the Scandinavians are concerned the forests are 'green gold'.

The taiga forests are especially noted for their production of softwoods such as pine and spruce. But hardwoods such as beech and birch also grow.

Softwoods grow and mature three to four times more quickly than hardwoods. The lumber industry is therefore able to harvest a softwood forest more frequently.

In the nineteenth century lumbering was a 'robber economy' with large areas of forest being cut and destroyed and no young trees planted to replace them. Today countries have a re-planting and conservation policy to make sure that this valuable resource is not used up.

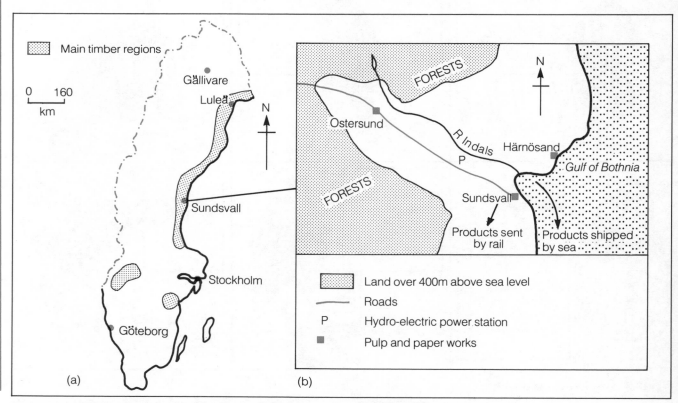

Fig. 14.1 (a) The timber regions of Sweden and **(b)** forestry in central Sweden

Fig. 14.2
Logs being
transported by
floating

14.4 Forestry in central Sweden

Opposite you can see a map of a timber producing area in central Sweden. At one time the trees were cut in the autumn and winter and then dragged to frozen rivers. When the river melted in the spring the logs floated down the river to the sawmills. Today most of the timber is carried by road. This is because:

1 the rivers are frozen for five months in the year;

2 the development of hydro-electric power stations has interrupted the flow of the rivers. Hydro-electricity provides cheap power for the sawmills and workshops.

Most of the timber is used to make pulp for the newsprint industry. Sawn timber for the building and furniture industries is also produced together with plywood, chipboard and matchwood.

Fig. 14.3 Products of the taiga

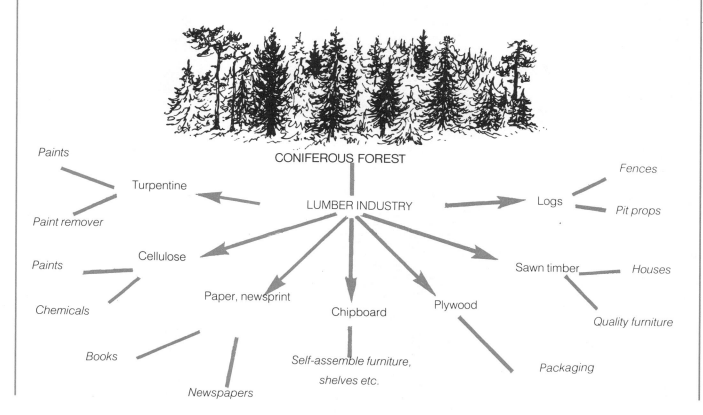

CONIFEROUS FOREST

Paints

Turpentine

Paint remover

LUMBER INDUSTRY

Fences

Logs

Pit props

Paints

Cellulose

Chemicals

Paper, newsprint

Chipboard

Plywood

Sawn timber

Houses

Quality furniture

Books

Newspapers

*Self-assemble furniture,
shelves etc.*

Packaging

Activities

A The picture diagram above shows the chief uses of the softwood timber after it has been cut down and processed.

(a) Copy out the diagram into your notebook leaving out the illustrations.

(b) Find out what each of the following are: chipboard, plywood, pit props. Write out a definition of each.

(c) Make a list of the products shown in the diagram which you can find in your own home and garden.

B Table 14.1 shows factors which favour the development of the lumber industry.

Factors favouring the lumber industry	How it applies to the Sundsvall region
Large forest resources	
Means of transporting logs to the mills	
Power for processing the timber	
Water for transport and for use in pulping mills	
Communications to get the products to market	

Table 14.1

Study Fig. 14.1(b) and complete the right-hand side of the table.

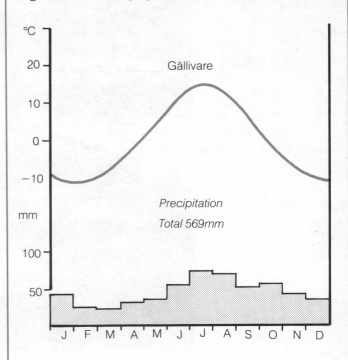

Fig. 14.4 A climate graph for Gällivare, Sweden

C Fig. 14.4 is a climate graph for Gällivare in the northern taiga lands of Sweden. Study the graph and answer the questions below.

(a) Which is the hottest month?

(b) Which is the coldest month?

(c) In how many months of the year is the average temperature below freezing?

(d) What is the annual range in temperature?

(e) Which are the wettest months?

(f) Which season of the year has the most rainfall?

(g) Write notes on the advantages and disadvantages of the climate for the forestry industry.

Unit 15

Continental grasslands

15.1 Introduction

Huge grassland areas are found in the interiors of continents in temperate latitudes. In Europe the chief continental grassland areas are the Steppes of the USSR.

15.2 Climate of the Steppes

Because the areas of grassland are far away from the influence of oceans, the land heats up quickly in summer and cools down quickly in winter. So the annual range in temperature is high.

Rain falls mainly in the summer when the heat of the land causes convection currents in the air and convectional rain. Since the lands are remote from the ocean the air does not contain much moisture and rainfall totals are low.

Summer temperatures rise to an average of 21°C in July. In winter two or three months have average temperatures below freezing point. But winters are shorter than in the taiga lands further north.

Fig. 15.2 Planting wheat on a collective farm in the USSR

The wetter parts of the grasslands have about 500 mm rainfall a year, most in summer thunderstorms. The drier parts have only half that amount a year. The lower the rainfall total the less reliable the rainfall is. In the drier areas there can be long periods of drought.

15.3 Soils of the Steppes

The most typical soil of the continental grassland regions is the fertile 'black earth'. It is also called

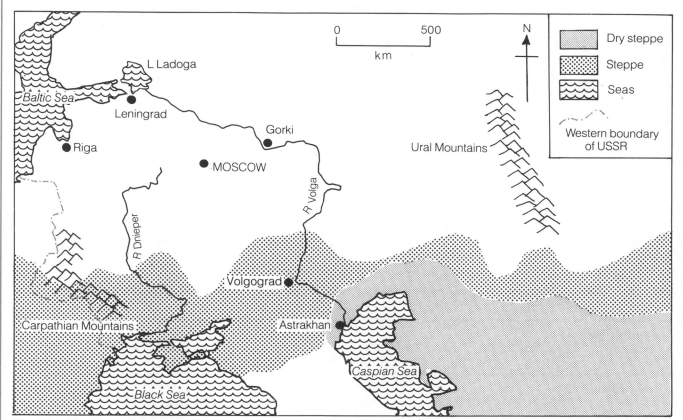

Fig. 15.1 The Steppe lands of USSR

a **chernozem**. Chernozems are rich in humus which is formed from decaying grass. Because it is very fertile the soil is ideal for growing grain.

15.4 Vegetation of the Steppes

These regions do not get enough precipitation to allow trees or bushes to grow. Willow and alder trees grow where they can find additional moisture – on the banks of rivers and around the edges of lakes. The main plant is grass. It grows in tufts and is dry, coarse and greyish in colour.

15.5 The Steppes of Russia

The open country of the Steppes has no shelter in winter from the bitter winds from Siberia, so this is a harsh season. The farmers plough their land in the autumn before the snow and heavy frosts come. They make full use of the very fertile soil and the Steppe lands are one of the most important farming regions in the USSR. The important crops are cereals, especially wheat, sugar beet, tobacco, fruit and sunflower seeds.

The southern lands around the Caspian Sea form the dry Steppe and have little rainfall. Irrigation schemes have now made it possible to grow crops. The driest areas are grazed by sheep and goats.

Activities

A Table 15.1 gives the climate data for two Russian cities. Odessa is on the Black Sea and on the south-west edge of the Steppes. Astrakhan lies further east on the Caspian Sea and is in the dry Steppes.

(a) Study the rainfall figures.
 (i) Which city has the more precipitation?
 (ii) Which is the wettest month in Astrakhan?
 (iii) In which season of the year does Odessa get most rain?
 (iv) Is this also true for Astrakhan?
 (v) Give one reason why Astrakhan has a drier climate than Odessa.

(b) Now look at the temperature figures.
 (i) Which city has the higher average summer temperatures?
 (ii) For how many months is the average temperature below freezing in Astrakhan?

(iii) Which city has the lower average winter temperatures?
(iv) Give one reason why Astrakhan has a higher range in temperature.
 (v) Draw temperature and rainfall graphs for both cities using the figures given in Table 15.1.

B Fig. 15.3 and Table 15.2 give you information on how the cultivated land in the USSR is used.

Fig. 15.3 Pie graph to show sown areas of crops in the USSR

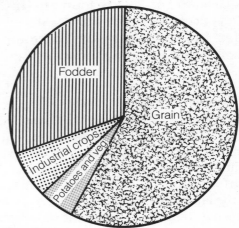

(a) In Fig. 15.3:
 (i) what is meant by industrial crops?
 (ii) Give one example of an industrial crop.
 (iii) Which of these statements is correct:
  grain takes up three-quarters of the cultivated land in Russia;
  over half the ploughed land in Russia is sown with grain;
  less than one-third of Russia's cultivated land is used for grain?
(b) **(i)** Use the figures in Table 15.2 to make a pie graph like the one in Fig. 15.3.
  (ii) Write notes on what your pie graph shows.

Crop	% of land used for growing grain
Wheat	47
Barley	27
Oats	9
Rye	7
Others	10

Table 15.2 Sown areas of grain crops in USSR

	J	F	M	A	M	J	J	A	S	O	N	D	
Rainfall (mm)													**Total**
Odessa	23	18	28	28	33	58	53	30	36	28	41	33	409
Astrakhan	13	8	10	13	15	18	13	13	13	10	10	13	149
Temperature (°C)													**Range**
Odessa	−3.1	−1.6	2.5	8.4	15.7	19.9	22.7	21.8	16.8	11.3	4.6	0.0	25.8
Astrakhan	−7.1	−5.1	0.4	8.8	17.6	22.6	25.4	23.2	16.9	9.7	2.2	−3.2	30.6

Table 15.1

Unit 16

The Mediterranean lands

16.1 Introduction

Fig. 16.1 below shows the countries around the Mediterranean Sea. These are the countries which many people believe to have an 'ideal' climate. It is said that people live better and enjoy themselves more in this climate than they do in any other climate in the world.

16.2 General features of the Mediterranean climate

The Mediterranean climate is a warm temperate one with the average monthly temperatures ranging from 10°C in January to 24°C in July.

These lands have two main seasons – a hot, dry summer and a cool wet winter. This pattern is the result of the fact that the region is dominated in winter by the westerly winds accompanied by depressions, and in the summer by the Azores high-pressure system.

Rainfall is moderate, about 750 mm a year. The rain is concentrated in fewer than 100 days a year. In the south of France there are about two months of drought in the summer. At the eastern end of the Mediterranean Sea the summer drought may last six months.

The lands around the Mediterranean Sea are characterized by islands, peninsulas, narrow coastal lowlands which rise suddenly to high mountains and inland basins. Because of this variety of landform the climate also varies from one locality to another. So, the broad pattern of the climate hides many local differences.

16.3 Vegetation of the Mediterranean lands

Mediterranean trees and plants are **xerophytic**, that is, they can withstand drought. The trees have long roots with which they can reach water deep in the ground. They also have thick bark which cuts down the amount of moisture given off (transpired) into the air.

There are also other ways in which the plants adapt. Some have shiny or wax-coated leaves which also cut down transpiration. The pine trees have narrow leaves so that there is little surface area for the sun to heat and cause transpiration. Many plants are succulents or have thick leaves in which moisture can be stored.

In the drier areas there is a scrub vegetation called maquis. This is made up of evergreen shrubs such as laurel, myrtle and rosemary.

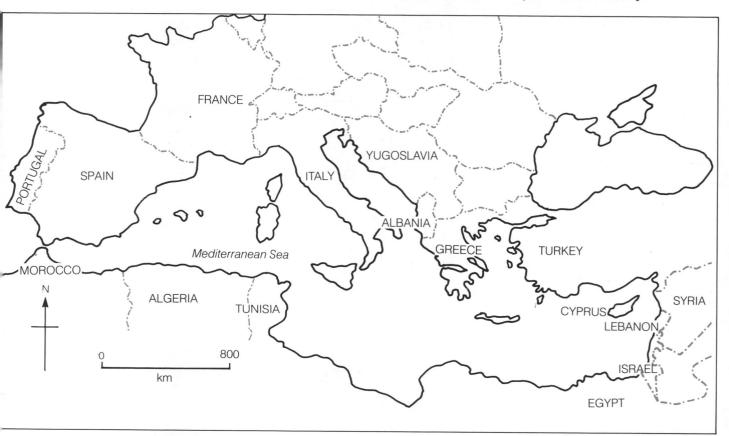

Fig. 16.1 The Mediterranean countries

48

Mediterranean trees and plants are evergreen. The winters are mild enough for this. Unlike the northern regions of Europe the summer is the season of rest for plants and trees, although many grow a little if moisture is available.

Activities

A The countries around the Mediterranean are very popular holiday regions. Below is a photo and sketch map of a famous Italian holiday centre – Sorrento in the Bay of Naples.

(a) Make a list of the things shown in the diagram which holidaymakers would find attractive.

(b) Write an account of how you would spend a day in Sorrento.

(c) Some people prefer sightseeing to sunbathing. Would Sorrento be a good place for them to visit? Give your reasons.

Fig. 16.2 The Corsican landscape

Fig. 16.3 Sorrento in the Bay of Naples

Fig. 16.4

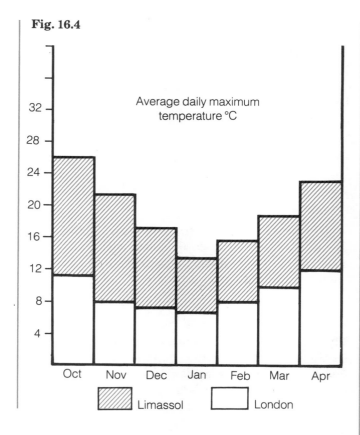

Average daily maximum temperature °C

Limassol London

B Fig. 16.4 and Table 16.1 show the kinds of information you can find in holiday brochures for Mediterranean countries.

(a) Look at the graph for Limassol:

  (i) Why is the temperature of Limassol compared with that of London?

 (ii) In which of the months shown is the difference between Limassol and London the greatest?

(iii) What does the graph **not** tell holidaymakers about the winter climate at Limassol?

(b) Now look at the figures for Corsica in Table 16.1.

	Average daytime temperature °C	Average hours of sunshine per day	Average sea temperatures °C
Jan.	12.8	4.2	13.3
Feb.	13.9	4.7	13.3
March	15.0	6.3	12.8
April	18.9	7.7	12.8
May	22.2	9.6	16.7
June	26.1	11.1	19.4
July	29.4	12.3	22.2
Aug.	29.4	10.9	23.3
Sept.	27.2	8.8	22.8
Oct.	21.7	8.8	20.0
Nov.	17.2	4.7	17.8
Dec.	14.4	3.3	15.0

Table 16.1 Climate data for Corsica

  (i) Draw one graph using three different lines to show the three sets of figures.

 (ii) Do the highest daytime temperatures, warmest sea temperatures and highest sunshine average all occur in the same month?

(iii) Write notes on what your graph shows.

(iv) Explain why the holiday season in Corsica begins in May and finishes at the end of October using the data in the table.

Unit 17

Farming in Europe

17.1 Introduction

Over 270 million people live in the EEC countries and, although Western Europe is regarded as one of the chief industrial regions of the world, it remains an important farming region.

The type of farming practised throughout Europe varies significantly. The two main factors causing the differences are:

1 variations in climate;
2 the different political and economic systems in Eastern and Western Europe.

17.2 General patterns of farming

Fig. 17.1 shows a very general picture of farming in Europe. Within each of the main regions shown there are areas which are different from the general pattern. You must also remember that the boundaries between the regions are not hard and fast divisions. One major type of land use gradually gives way to another.

The map shows the influence of climate.

1 The unproductive lands are the wastelands of the tundra (Unit 13). It is too cold for farming in the northern mountains of Scandinavia.

2 In the forest lands which lie to the south of the tundra the very cold winters, short growing season and infertile soils limit farming.

3 The pastoral areas are mainly uplands and moorlands. The thin soils, steep slopes and often wet conditions do not favour arable farming. The wet western maritime areas also belong to this category.

4 The arable lands are those lands which most favour farming. Most are lowlands with fertile soils and climates which give warm summers and enough rainfall to grow crops.

17.3 Types of farming

The north-west European type is found in Britain and neighbouring countries. It is also found around the Baltic Sea. Most of the farming is commercial with the farms providing food and the raw materials needed by the industrial regions and cities. Much capital is invested in the farms which use modern machinery and scientific farming techniques.

The Mediterranean type is a farming type in which the winter half of the year is the busier. Wheat and barley are sown in the autumn. Wheat is the most typical farm crop together with vines and olives. Because of the summer drought the growing of grass is far less important than in northern Europe. Traditional methods of farming are still widespread as you will see in Unit 19.

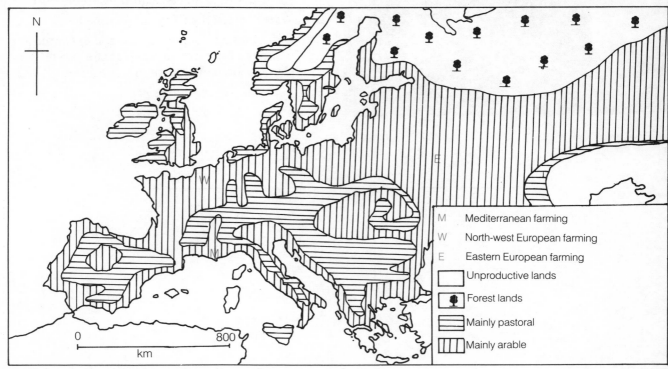

M	Mediterranean farming
W	North-west European farming
E	Eastern European farming
	Unproductive lands
	Forest lands
	Mainly pastoral
	Mainly arable

Fig. 17.1 Types of farming in Europe

Fig. 17.2 A farm on the Isle of Fünen, Denmark

The Eastern European type does not have the mixture of crops found on most farms in the west. There is greater concentration on a few crops to which the region is especially suited. Traditionally Eastern Europe was a region of peasant farming with families working small farms for subsistence.

A revolution has occurred in farming since the coming of communism. Eastern Europe now has many collective farms (Unit 22).

Activities

A Write a description of what Fig. 17.2 shows.

B Many people assume that countries with a high proportion of people still working on the land are characterized by low wages and poverty.

The measure we use to show how wealthy a country is is the **Gross Domestic Product (GDP)** per head of population. We can test whether there is a relationship between prosperity and the proportion of the population who farm by using a **scatter graph**.

Country	GDP per head per year (Eur. Curr Units)	Rank A	% of pop. employed on farms	Rank B
Fed. Rep. Germany (FG)	8189		6.2	
France (F)	6941		8.8	
Italy (I)	3597		14.8	
Netherlands (N)	7338		4.8	
Belgium (B)	7551		3.2	
Luxembourg (L)	7777		6.1	
United Kingdom (UK)	4347		2.6	
Rep. Ireland (RI)	2878		21.0	
Denmark (D)	8627	2	8.3	
Greece (G)	2634		30.8	1
Spain (Sp)	3207		19.5	
Portugal (P)	1428		30.6	2
Norway (No)	7753		8.6	
Sweden (Sw)	8253	3	5.8	
Switzerland (Sz)	10 539	1	7.6	

Table 17.1

Activities continued

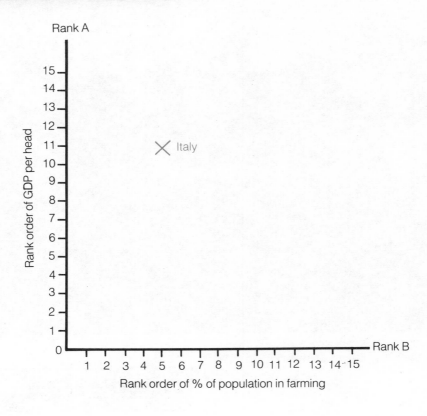

Fig. 17.3 Rank order of the percentage of population in farming

(a) Copy out Table 17.1.

(b) In the column marked 'Rank A' rank the figures for GDP from highest to lowest – you have been given a start.

(c) Rank the percentage of farm population in the same way in Rank B.

(d) Draw the frame of a graph like Fig. 17.3.

(e) Plot the rank numbers (columns A and B) for each country. Italy has been done for you.

(f) Mark the point which represents the country with the initial letter(s) shown in the table.

(g) With Fig. 17.4 as a guide draw around the dots.

(h) Which of the diagrams in Fig. 17.4 – a, b, or c – looks most like your graph?

Fig. 17.4 shows whether there is a relationship (link) between the proportion of the population in farming and wealth in European countries.

In a – in general, wealthy countries have the highest proportion of farming population.

In b – in general, the wealthiest countries have the smallest proportion of farming population.

In c – there is no link between the two.

(i) What does your graph show?

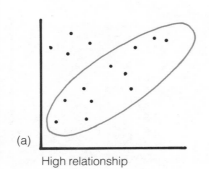

(a) High relationship

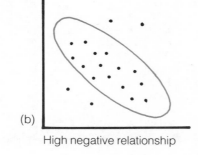

(b) High negative relationship

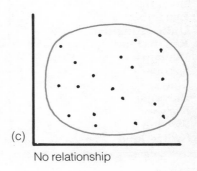

(c) No relationship

Fig. 17.4

Unit 18

Farming the marginal lands

18.1 What do we mean by marginal land?

In many countries only some of the land is suitable for farming. In some places such as in Snowdonia and the Highlands of Scotland the bare rock and thin acid soils make farming impossible over large areas. The climate can also make farming difficult; some places are too wet and others are too cool for crops to grow well. These lands are known as marginal lands because the land is only marginally suitable for farming. Most of the land is so unproductive that the farmers who work there only just manage to make a living.

18.2 Farming in Norway

As far as farming is concerned Norway is largely marginal land. There are three main reasons for this.

Relief Norway is a mountainous country and there is little lowland suitable for farming.

Soils The ancient resistant rocks of Norway break down into infertile soils. Glaciers also scraped away much of the soil in the valleys.

Climate Norway has a cool temperate climate which gradually changes into a polar climate northwards. Summers are too cool and wet for many crops. Wheat, for example, can only be grown in the south-east of the country.

Fig. 18.1 shows how the land is used for farming in the southern fjords. Since there is so little, lowland farm villages are found in isolated pockets.

Most farms are small—less than 10 hectares in area. Most farms are worked by the farmer and his family. Very little is sold off the farm for cash. Most of the farmland is used to produce fodder crops for animals, especially dairy cattle.

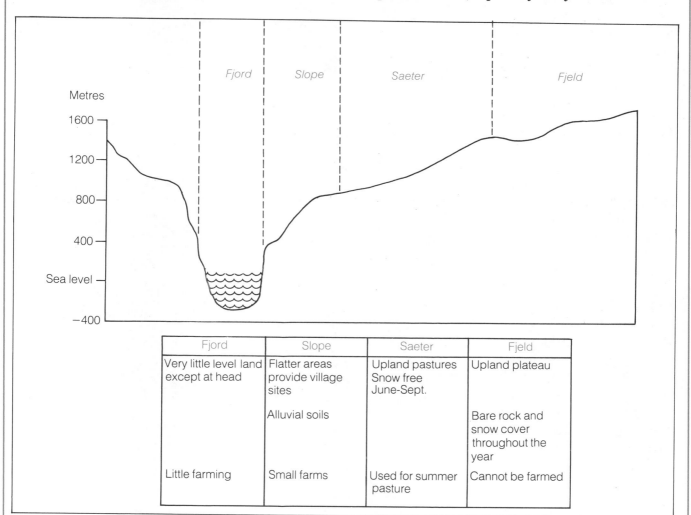

Fjord	Slope	Saeter	Fjeld
Very little level land except at head	Flatter areas provide village sites	Upland pastures Snow free June-Sept.	Upland plateau
	Alluvial soils		Bare rock and snow cover throughout the year
Little farming	Small farms	Used for summer pasture	Cannot be farmed

Fig. 18.1 A cross-section of a fjord

54

Transhumance

Farmers in Norway have to make use of all the pasture they can. When the snow has melted on the mountains the **saeter** or upland meadows (Fig. 18.1) provide good pasture from June to September for the dairy cows. The farmer takes his herd up to the saeter where traditionally milk was made into cheese.

The movement of farm animals from one climate zone to another as a regular part of the farming year is called transhumance.

Activities

A Fig. 18.2 shows a farm village located high above a fjord in Norway. Hay is drying on racks in the fields around the village.

(a) Put some tracing paper over the photograph and trace around the shapes of the mountains and the fjord.

(b) Mark on your tracing:
  (i) the location of the village;
 (ii) the position of the fields;
(iii) a road along the fjord shore.

(c) Label your sketch to show these features.

(d) Why are there very few farm fields in the photo?

(e) What is the advantage of putting the hay on racks to dry?

(f) What is the hay needed for?

B Imagine you are a journalist who is writing an article about farming in Norway. You have interviewed farmers about how they use the saeter in summer. Here are four of the things the farmers told you:

(a) It is too much trouble to take the cows up the mountain to the saeter. I feed them on cattle cake as well as hay so they keep in good condition.

(b) I have modernized my saeter house and let it to foreign tourists in the summer.

(c) Since they built the new road to the saeter we don't make cheese in summer. A lorry collects our milk every day for the creamery.

(d) I have sold my summer farm on the saeter to city people for a week-end cottage.

Write your newspaper article with the title 'Old ways are disappearing from the countryside'.

Fig. 18.2 Geiranger, Norway

Fig. 18.3

Unit 19

Mediterranean fruit farming

Fig. 19.2

19.1 Introduction

Italy is an excellent example of a Mediterranean farming country with its emphasis upon the production of wine, wheat and olives, as the most typical products.

Italy is the second largest producer of grapes in the world and produces more wine than any other European country. It is also first in the world in the production of olive oil. Cereal crops are important throughout the country and especially so in the north. The chief cereal by far is wheat which makes up 70 per cent of the total production of all grain in Italy. It is used to make the famous pastas like spaghetti.

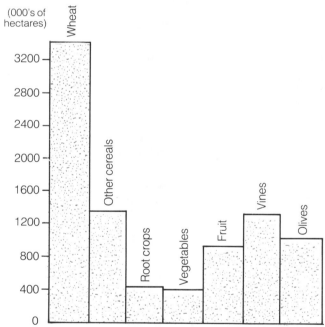

Fig. 19.1 How the land is used for important crops in Italy

19.2 Fruit and olives in Italy

Fig. 19.1 above shows the amounts of land devoted to different crops in Italy. Although wheat is shown as the chief single crop, if the fruit and vegetables, olives and vines, are added together, they exceed the area which is used for wheat.

Grapes are grown all over Italy and every region produces its own wines. Many of these are for local use. The average consumption of wine in

Italy is 130 bottles per person per year. Since 1960 the Italians have tried to control the quality of the wines produced, especially those for export. Some Italian wines such as Chianti, Asti Spumante and Soave have become very well known in other European countries.

The vines provide about 10 per cent of Italy's income from farming. Nearly 4 million people are employed in viticulture (vine growing) and wine making. Most of the production comes from small farms – over 50 per cent from farms of less than 10 hectares in area.

Other fruits are also important crops. Sicily is noted especially for lemons and oranges. On the mainland, lemon and orange groves are found mainly south of Naples. Further north fruits which can be grown in cooler climates become important – apples, pears and cherries.

Olives only grow in a climate with hot (20° – 28°C), dry summers and mild winters. The peninsula of Italy is very well suited to the crop. In Britain we see olives in salads, or stuffed to be eaten with certain drinks. But the chief use of the olive in Mediterranean lands is to provide cooking oil.

19.3 Other Mediterranean lands

Like Italy, both Spain and Portugal produce large quantities of grapes and wine. Spain is famous for sherry, Portugal for port. Other fruits are also important. The United Kingdom imports Spanish Seville oranges to make marmalade. The chief producer of quality wine is France south of the River Loire. The other Mediterranean country in the EEC, Greece, also produces a range of wines, lemons, oranges and olive oil.

Activities

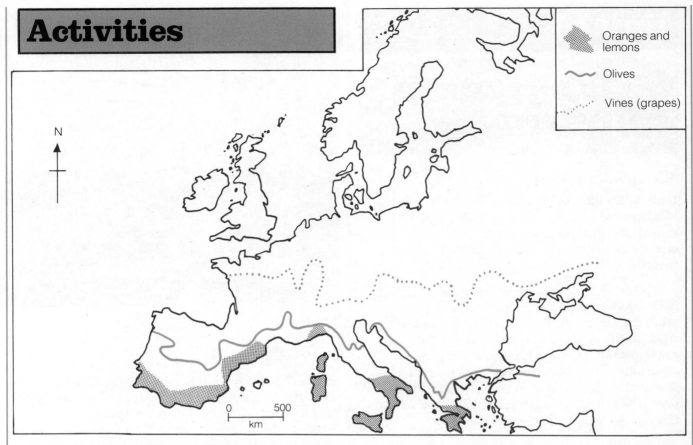

Legend:
- Oranges and lemons
- Olives
- Vines (grapes)

N

A Fig. 19.3 shows the usual northern limits for the cultivation of typical products of Mediterranean farms.

(a) Describe the pattern it shows.

(b) With Spain and Portugal in the EEC some other countries fear that there will be a huge wine surplus. How many EEC countries are major wine producers?

(c) For which of the crops shown is France **not** a very important producer?

B Below are details of a farm in Italy. The farm is near the city of Perugia in Umbria.

Fig. 19.3 Northern limits of crop production in southern Europe

(a) How can you tell from the details that the cows are milked by hand?

(b) Why do you think the old lady believes it is not worth buying a milking machine?

(c) Why is hay an important crop on the farm?

(d) Name two cash crops produced by this farm.

(e) Which crops are grown for the family's own use?

(f) Explain why neighbours have left their farming homes and sold them to city people for weekend cottages.

Area	25 hectares
Owner	elderly widow
Labour	owner + son, his wife and one daughter
Stock	6 cows, 25 sheep, 500 chickens
Crops	Hay, sugar beet vegetables – beans, peppers, aubergines olive oil grapes for wine

Machinery 1 tractor

Produce for sale
eggs, cheese, vegetables
180 litres of milk per day
calves

Markets
milk – creamery in Perugia
cheese – local shop
vegetables – Perugia market
sugar beet – processing factory
calves – local butcher

Problems Costs of animal food and pesticides are rising
Milk prices are not going up
People eat fewer eggs, so they are harder to sell
Working hours are very long (4.30 a.m. start in summer)
Family income from the farm is low

Unit 20

Grain cultivation

20.1 Introduction

The chief kind of food eaten by man comes from cultivated grasses. The heads of different kinds of grasses are called cereals. The most commonly eaten cereal in the world is rice, but in the western world wheat is by far the most important.

In the world as a whole about 160 million hectares of land are used to grow wheat. This is a greater area than is used for any other cereal.

Western Europe is one of the chief wheat producing areas in the world. Other cereals are also grown in Europe – maize, oats, rye and, in a few isolated pockets, rice.

20.2 Conditions necessary for the production of grain in Europe

Wheat grows well in the temperate lands of Europe. It requires 90 days a year when the temperature is over 5.6°C and grows best in areas with moderate rainfall – 500 to 700 mm a year. Heavy loam and clay soils are ideal, but the soils need to be well drained so that machinery can be used on the land.

Maize needs a warmer climate than wheat and grows best in the subtropical areas. It needs 140 days with a temperature of 6.0°C or over. It also needs 625 to 1025 mm of rainfall during the summer months when it is growing fastest. The soils have to be warm and rich.

Barley likes the same growing conditions as wheat but it will also grow well in light soils. Barley can also survive better in poor weather than wheat.

Oats and **rye** will grow in the poorer, cooler lands. Rye likes best the conditions which favour wheat but will put up with poorer soils and will ripen in cooler, wetter summers. Oats will also grow in cooler lands. Oats can put up with rainy, cloudy summers.

20.3 Grain farming in Spain and Portugal

The Iberian Peninsula is suitable for cereal growing except for the fact that most of the area has an arid climate. In the Meseta, the central plain, rainfall may be less than 300 mm a year.

Fig. 20.1 Scything wheat in northern Spain

There is also less rain in the hot summer than in the winter months.

Like farmers in other arid regions the farmers of the dry parts of Spain practise **dry farming**. Dry farming is a way of catching every drop of moisture possible in the soil. A crop is grown one year and then the land is left fallow (unused); in that year the soil is ploughed to turn the moisture into the ground to store it for the next crop.

The north and west of the Iberian Peninsula have a much moister climate so maize can be grown in these regions.

Fig. 20.2 Maize being checked for ripeness

Activities

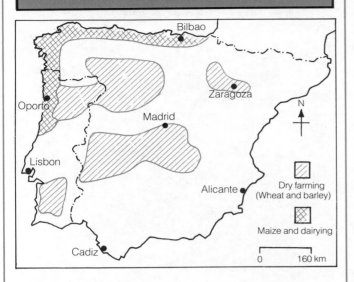

Fig. 20.3 Important cereal growing areas of the Iberian Peninsula

A Study Fig. 20.3 and answer these questions:

(a) How can you tell from the map that the interior of Spain has little rainfall each year?

(b) Wheat is used to make flour. How is barley used – (an encyclopaedia may help)?

(c) What climatic factor makes maize growing and dairying go well together in the north-west of Spain?

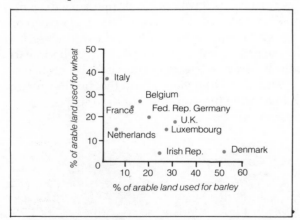

Fig. 20.4 A scatter diagram of the percentage of arable land used for wheat and barley in European countries

B Fig. 20.4 is a scatter diagram which shows the percentage of arable land used for wheat and barley in nine EEC countries.

(a) Which country has the highest proportion of arable land devoted to wheat?

(b) Which has the highest proportion devoted to barley?

(c) Name the EEC countries which have a greater proportion of land devoted to growing wheat than barley.

C Turn back to the Activities in Unit 17 page 51; Fig. 17.5. It will help you answer these two questions:

(a) Does the scatter diagram in Fig. 20.4 show a high relationship, a high negative relationship or no relationship at all?

(b) Which of the following statements is true?

  (i) Countries with a high proportion of land in wheat usually also have a high proportion of land in barley.

  (ii) Generally countries with a high proportion of arable land in wheat have a low proportion of their arable land in barley.

  (iii) There is no link (relationship) between the two crops.

D Table 20.1 shows rounded up totals for cereal production in seven European countries in a recent year. Study the table.

(a) Which of the countries is by far the greatest producer of cereals?

(b) Give reasons to explain each of the following facts:

  (i) Norway grows few cereals.

  (ii) Oats are an important crop in Norway.

  (iii) France is an important producer of grain.

  (iv) The United Kingdom does not grow rye.

(c) Draw bar graphs to show cereal production in Spain and Denmark using the figures in the table.

(d) Give reasons for the differences you note in the graphs.

Country	Wheat	Rye	Barley	Oats	Maize	Total of all grain crops
Fed. Rep. of Germany	7500	2500	7500	3500	500	24 500
France	18 000	500	9750	2250	7500	38 000
United Kingdom	5500	—	9500	1000	—	16 000
Denmark	500	250	6000	250	—	7 000
Spain	4500	250	6750	500	1750	14 000
Norway	—	—	500	500	—	1 000
USSR	103 000	13 000	61 500	18 500	10 000	209 000

Table 20.1 Production of cereals in Europe (000's of tonnes)

Unit 21

Land reclamation

21.1 Introduction

Land reclamation is the making of flooded or waste land suitable for farming and for other uses. The European country in which most reclamation has taken place is the Netherlands which we sometimes call Holland.

In other countries too important reclamation schemes have been completed. In Denmark, for example, at one time only 40 per cent of the Jutland Peninsula could be farmed. Today nearly all the land is fit to use for farming. Deep ploughing has improved drainage and the addition of lime, which is alkaline, has cut down the acidity of the soil. Trees and grass have been planted to fix the sand dunes. Former wastelands are now useful cattle rearing areas.

21.2 Land reclamation in the Netherlands

The cartoon below illustrates an old story but it is no joke. The Great Floods of 1953 killed 1800 people. Keeping the sea defences of the Netherlands in good order is an important task for the Dutch. They are even more concerned with increasing the amount of land they have, by reclaiming it from the sea.

A piece of land which has been reclaimed in this way is called a **polder**. The submerged land which is to be recovered is surrounded by a dyke. The water is then pumped out into canals surrounding the area. In the old days the power for the pumps was provided by windmills. Today powerful pumps which control the flow of water are run by electricity.

Without land reclamation most of the Netherlands would be under water or marshland. At one time the length of the Dutch coastline was nearly 2000 km. Thirty years ago reclamation schemes had reduced it to 1300 km. The aim is to get it down to 500 km. There have been two main projects in the last fifty years. The first was the reclaiming of the Zuider Zee. The newest project is the Delta Plan. After the Great Floods the chief concern of the Delta Plan is to make the land safer from big floods.

The Dutch have also improved poor heathland areas called **geest**. During the last hundred years much work has been done to turn them into mixed farming areas. The Dutch used the same methods as the Danes in Jutland. Some of the Dutch heathland which still remains is now used for leisure parks.

Activities

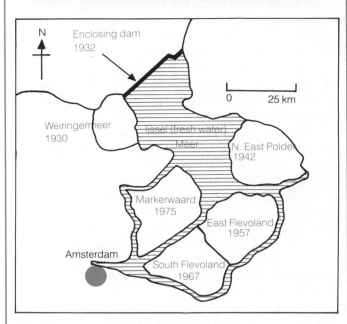

Fig. 21.1 Reclamation of the Zuider Zee

A Fig. 21.1 shows the stages in which the Zuider Zee was reclaimed.

(a) Copy the map into your book.

(b) Use shading and a key to show the stages of reclamation.

B Fig. 21.3 opposite shows a village on the North-East Polder from the air.

(a) What are the shapes of the fields?

(b) How many farms can you see in the photograph?

(c) Why is each farm surrounded by trees?

(d) Why was it easy to make the roads so straight?

(e) Draw a plan to show the pattern of settlement on the polder.

C Fig. 21.2 shows a cross-section of the polder lands of Holland.

(a) Why do the engineers have to take the storm level of the North Sea into account?

(b) How can you tell from the diagram that the Zuider Zee was a submerged area?

(c) From the diagram explain how the water is controlled in the polder lands.

(d) Why are canals needed in the polder lands?

(e) Explain what an 'enclosing dam' is (Fig. 21.1 will help).

D In making a polder the engineers have to follow a number of important steps. Below are eight of the steps which they have to take. They are not arranged in the correct order.

Read each of the statements and then rearrange them in the correct sequence. Write them out in your notebook in the correct order.

    A After five years farming starts

    B Part of the shallow lake is shut off with a dyke

    C Water behind the dam is let out through the gates at low tide

    D Drainage ditches and canals are dug

    E Pumping stations are built

    F Water is pumped out of the shut-off part

    G New land is sown with reeds to help soil form

    H An enclosing dam is built to shut off the bay from the sea

Fig. 21.3 A planned village in the North-East Polder of the Zuider Zee

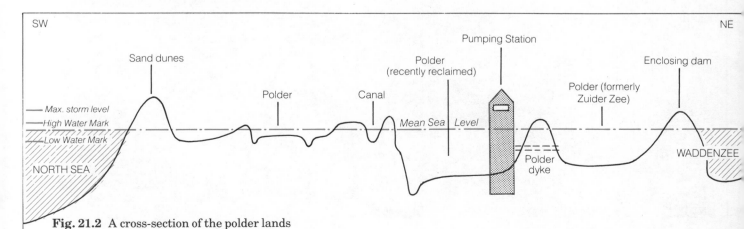

Fig. 21.2 A cross-section of the polder lands

Unit 22

Farming in Eastern Europe

22.1 Introduction

The countries of Eastern Europe have communist systems of government. As far as farming is concerned this creates many differences in the way in which farming is organized compared with farming in Britain and other Western countries.

There are three important facts to remember:

1 Land in Eastern Europe is not owned by individual people or families but by the state (the country).

2 Farming is organized on a collective basis (see below).

3 Farming is directed and organized in most communist countries by government planners.

22.2 Collective farming

This is a system of farming in which the land is run according to plans thought out by the people who work on it. The farms are state controlled and are based on the idea that people get more satisfaction from working for the village than they would working for themselves.

The workers share the land, machinery and animals. They decide how money is to be shared out or spent. Together, they also decide who will do the various jobs on the farm.

The collective farm is expected to play its part in helping the country achieve a National Plan. These National Plans usually last for five years.

Decisions are made on the farm by elected committees and by the votes of the workers.

The advantages of collective farming

(i) A group of workers can buy modern machinery which a single farmer could not afford.

(ii) By sharing work on a shift system the work is done more efficiently and the workers get more spare time.

(iii) Village fields can be grouped into bigger fields so that large modern machines can be used.

(iv) The collective farm can afford to train farm scientists and veterinary surgeons.

(v) Workshops and processing plants can be set up so that people in the village can work all through the year.

(vi) Some of the profits can be used by the community to build a village hall, a cinema, sports fields or other leisure facilities.

Fig. 22.1
Wheat harvesting in Georgia, USSR

Activities

Duties	Rights
To carry out the 'work units' agreed by the committee (the number of work days for the year)	To share in profits and produce according to the amount of work done
To take part in planning meetings	To have a say in making decisions
To give up an individual farm to become part of collective	To be paid for land and buildings put into the collective
To obey the managing committee	To have a private garden for growing food
To protect the property of the collective	To have the use of all leisure facilities on the collective

Table 22.1 Duties and rights of people on collective farms

A Above are some typical duties and rights of a farmworker on a collective farm in Eastern Europe.

(a) Why does the farmworker need to grow his own vegetables?

(b) How is working time measured?

(c) Why do some workers feel that they have lost their freedom?

(d) Do you think it a good idea that his share of the profits depends upon the amount of work a man does?

B Fig. 22.2 shows the plan of a collective farm in Russia.

(a) Name two kinds of community buildings you might find in the centre of the village.

(b) The collective farm covers an area roughly 10 km long and 7.5 km wide. Why are there so many tracks from the village to the fields?

(c) What kinds of things will the villagers grow on the plots which lie behind their houses?

(d) Below is a list of the main items of machinery found on this collective:

$$\begin{array}{lr} \text{tractors} & 100 \\ \text{lorries} & 50 \\ \text{combine harvesters} & 9 \\ \text{sugar beet harvesters} & 6 \end{array}$$

(i) What does the machinery list tell us about what is grown on the collective?

(ii) What is a combine harvester used for?

(iii) Why does the village need to own lorries?

(iv) What is the advantage of having very large fields?

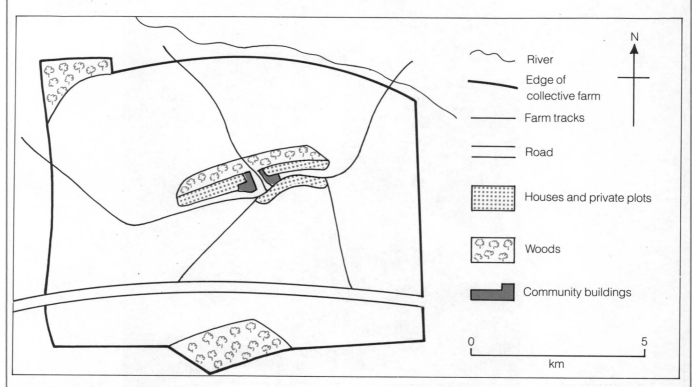

Fig. 22.2 A collective farm in Russia

Unit 23

Dairy farming in Denmark

23.1 Introduction

Denmark is a prosperous country with high living standards. Nearly one-third of its export trade is made up of farm produce – especially bacon, tinned pork, butter and cheese.

Denmark is a lowland country but it does not have very fertile soil. Because of the cold winters the animals have to be kept indoors in sheds, so fodder crops are very important arable crops on the farm (see Fig. 23.1).

The secret of Denmark's success as a farming country is that for many years the Danish farmers have kept their farms up-to-date, organized their farming efficiently and

have changed what they produce to match what other countries want to buy. One of the key factors in that success has been the system of cooperative farming.

Fig. 23.2 The main dairying areas of Denmark

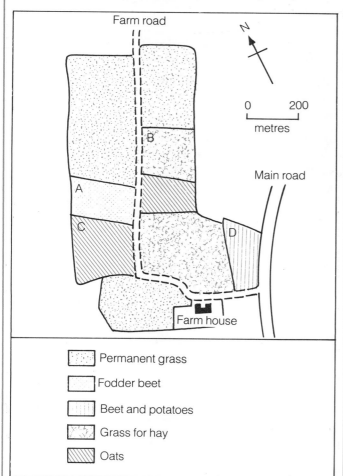

Fig. 23.1 A farm in Jutland

23.2 Cooperative farming

Danish farmers grouped themselves into cooperatives to get for themselves the kinds of advantages which large modern industries possess. Small farmers were able to keep their independence but, at the same time, they were able to increase their profits by working together. Overleaf are some of the advantages which the small farmers enjoyed when they became members of a cooperative.

In the cooperative the farmers learned modern methods. They shared the cost of buying machinery, lorries and equipment. Their milk could be processed in their own creameries and cheese factories. The quality of the butter, bacon and cheese was carefully controlled so that customers knew exactly what they were buying when they chose Danish products.

When Denmark joined the EEC with Britain, it was able to preserve its main markets and get the advantages of the Common Agricultural Policy (see Unit 24).

Fig. 23.3 Who does best?

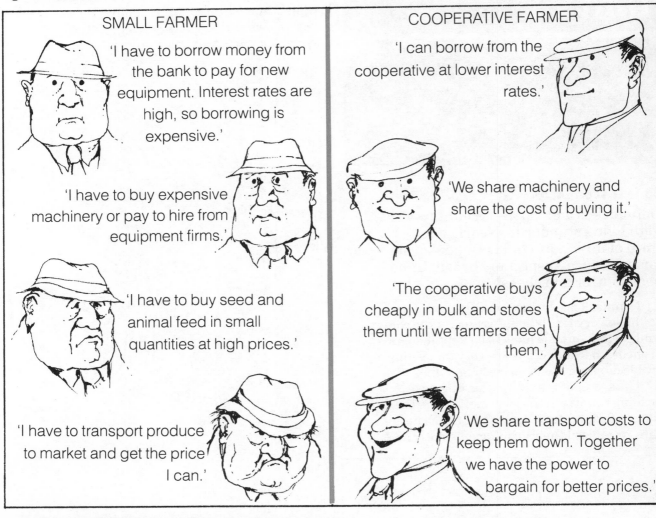

SMALL FARMER

'I have to borrow money from the bank to pay for new equipment. Interest rates are high, so borrowing is expensive.'

'I have to buy expensive machinery or pay to hire from equipment firms.'

'I have to buy seed and animal feed in small quantities at high prices.'

'I have to transport produce to market and get the price I can.'

COOPERATIVE FARMER

'I can borrow from the cooperative at lower interest rates.'

'We share machinery and share the cost of buying it.'

'The cooperative buys cheaply in bulk and stores them until we farmers need them.'

'We share transport costs to keep them down. Together we have the power to bargain for better prices.'

Activities

A Study the plan of the farm on the previous page. On the left-hand side you can see how the fields were used in one year. The farmer rotates his field crops in this order:

1 grass for hay
2 grain (rye)
3 fodder beet
4 grain (oats)
5 sugar beet and potatoes

(a) Name the crops in the rotation which will be grown in the following year in fields A, B, C and D.

(b) What is fodder beet grown for?

(c) Which crops are cash crops?

(d) Which fields are not included in the rotation?

B Fig. 23.4 shows the different types of land use in Denmark.

(a) What are the two chief uses?

(b) Which of the following crops could belong to the 'green fodder' group: potatoes, turnips, clover, hay.

(c) Name two cereals grown in Denmark.

(d) What is a 'root crop'?

C When you next visit a supermarket look for things we import from Denmark. Some clues – look at the meat, bacon, tinned meat and dairy counters in particular.

Make a list of what you find.

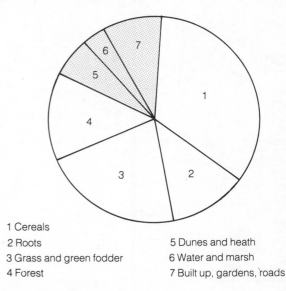

1 Cereals
2 Roots
3 Grass and green fodder
4 Forest
5 Dunes and heath
6 Water and marsh
7 Built up, gardens, roads

Fig. 23.4 Land use in Denmark

Unit 24

The Common Agricultural Policy

24.1 Background

In 1957, six Western European countries joined together in the European Economic Community (the EEC). We more often call it the Common Market. When they signed the Treaty of Rome the six countries agreed to work together, to reduce customs barriers between them and to work towards becoming politically united one day.

At first Britain stayed out of the EEC but in 1973 Britain, Denmark and the Irish Republic became members. Since then Greece, Portugal and Spain have joined.

24.2 The Common Agricultural Policy

One of the aims of the Treaty of Rome was to set up a Common Agricultural Policy (CAP) for all members. The intention was that CAP would:

1 increase the productivity of farms;
2 make sure that farmers and farm workers have a fair standard of living;
3 stabilize (steady) markets so that farmers would be sure that they could sell their produce;
4 make certain that the farmers produced the food supplies needed by EEC members;
5 make it certain that food reaches the shops at reasonable prices.

24.3 The effects of CAP

Since CAP has been in existence, farmers in the EEC countries have a better standard of living. In the Irish Republic, for example, the farmers are now much more prosperous than at any other time in their history. Farmers throughout the EEC are also certain that they can sell all they produce at good prices. So they are able to plan for the future with much greater confidence.

But CAP also has a number of disadvantages:

1 By guaranteeing prices for the farmers the EEC has made the price of food high. Food was cheap in Britain before it joined the Common Market, but the increase in the cost of food has made the EEC very unpopular with many British people.

2 Since the farmers are certain that they can sell their produce they produce more than is needed, or can be sold, outside the EEC. As a result there have been butter, meat, grain and wine surpluses – the so-called butter mountain, wine lake and so on. Expensive warehouses have had to be built to store the unwanted surpluses.

Fig. 24.1 EEC building in the centre of Brussels

3 As standards of living and costs have gone up the production costs of farmers have also risen. In the poorer farming areas this has put small farmers out of business.

Activities

A Name the countries numbered in Fig. 24.2.

B In Fig. 24.3 are comments made by six people about the Common Market (EEC).

(a) Which comment was made by a farmer who is doing well?

(b) Which comment was made by an EEC civil servant who is embarrassed by the surpluses?

(c) What effect has CAP had upon the old age pensioners' eating habits?

(d) Write comments which might be made by:

 (i) a housewife whose husband is unemployed;

 (ii) someone who manufactures artificial fertilizer;

(iii) a long-distance lorry driver with a refrigerated lorry.

C Table 24.1 shows the ways in which the EEC has dealt with some of the food surpluses produced by the Common Agricultural Policy.

Commodity	Solution(s)
Lamb	Stored in new refrigerated storehouses
Milk	Dried and stored Farmers given quota
Butter	Stored in refrigerated storehouses Sold cheaply to Eastern Europe Sold cheaply in supermarkets for a period of time, in the EEC
Wine	Turned into industrial alcohol Poured away
Grain	Stored Given to famine-affected countries

Table 24.1

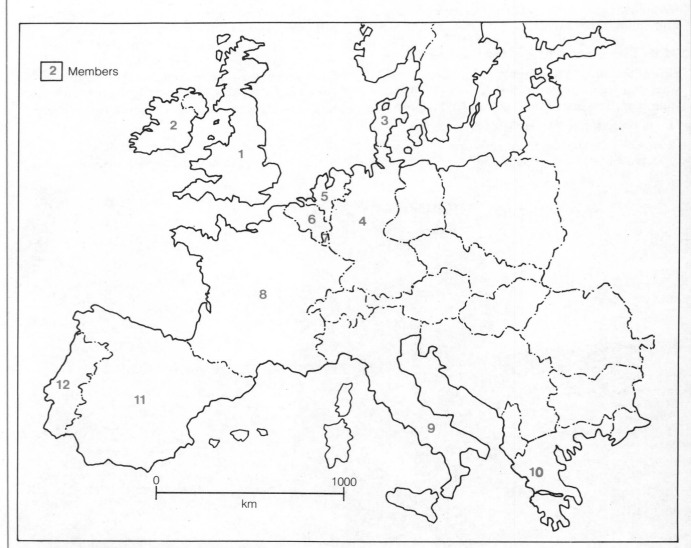

Fig. 24.2 The European Economic Community

Fig. 24.3

(a) Which are the two best solutions as far as you are concerned? Give your reasons.

(b) Why do some people believe that surpluses should not be sold cheaply to countries in Eastern Europe?

(c) Why do farmers dislike the idea of quotas which limit how much they can produce?

(d) In what ways can the dried milk be used?

(e) Have you any other ideas as to how surpluses could be dealt with?

Population and settlement

Unit 25

The population of Western Europe

25.1 Introduction

Fig. 25.1(a) shows the density of population for the countries of Western Europe. The chief feature is that the most densely populated countries are the 'low countries' of Belgium and the Netherlands. These two countries have one of the highest densities in the world – higher than that of Japan, but not as high as the densities reached in Hong Kong, Singapore and Bangladesh.

The Federal Republic of Germany and the United Kingdom are also densely populated countries.

The countries with the lowest densities are on the edges of Western Europe. They are said to be **peripheral**. Of the sparsely populated countries Eire (the Republic of Ireland) is the only country in Western Europe that has suffered an actual fall in population in the last 100 years.

25.2 Regional patterns

Within each country there are variations in the density of population from one part of the country to another.

The most densely populated areas and the emptiest regions of Western Europe are shown in Fig. 25.1(b). The most densely populated regions are the chief industrial regions of Western Europe. In Britain for example the belt of densest population stretches from Liverpool and industrial Lancashire to London and the south-east. On the continent the chief belt of dense population stretches from the mouth of the River Rhine to the Ruhr industrial region of Germany and the coalfields of Belgium and northern France.

The industrial regions of the Paris area and the North Italian industrial region also have high population densities.

In contrast, the emptiest areas can be accounted for by the physical character of the environment. The most empty are the high mountainous regions – the Alps, the Pyrenees, the Highlands of Scotland and the mountain backbone of Norway and Sweden.

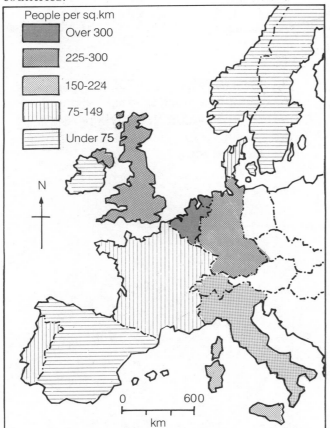

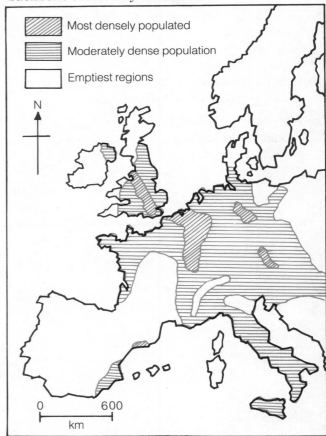

Fig. 25.1 Population density of Western Europe **(a)** by country and **(b)** by region

Activities

A Study Table 25.1 below.

Country	Population (millions)	Density (people p. sq km)
Fed. Republic of Germany	61.3	247
France	53.2	98
Italy	56.7	188
Republic of Ireland	3.3	47
Spain	36.7	73
Belgium	9.8	323
Netherlands	13.9	338
United Kingdom	55.9	229

Table 25.1

(a) Which of the countries shown has the greatest population?

(b) Is Belgium more or less crowded than West Germany?

(c) Which country has the fewest inhabitants per square kilometre?

(d) Which is the most densely populated country?

B The square shown in Fig. 25.2 represents 1 square kilometre. Each dot represents 10 people (to the nearest 10). The square represents the density of population in the Republic of Ireland. (47 = 50 to the nearest 10 persons per sq km.)

(a) Draw three squares of the same size.

(b) Use the squares to show the density of population (given in Table 25.1) of:
 (i) France
 (ii) United Kingdom
 (iii) Belgium

(c) Write sentences on the relationship between the size of the total population and the density in each of these three countries.

C The table below shows how it is expected the populations of different European countries will change. The population figures for 1985 and 1990 are **forecasts** or **projections**.

The percentage change from 1980 to 1990 is calculated:

$$\frac{\text{population forecast}}{\text{population 1980}} \times 100 = \% \text{ change}$$

Fig. 25.2

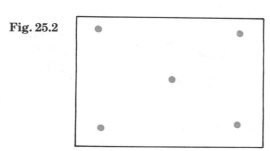

(a) For which country or countries would you say:
 (i) the population size is stable;
 (ii) the population will fall in the 10 years shown;
 (iii) rapid population growth is forecast?

(b) Fig. 25.3 is the start of a graph showing the figures in the final column of Table 25.2.
 (i) Complete this graph in your file or exercise book.
 (ii) Write brief notes on what the graph shows.

Fig. 25.3

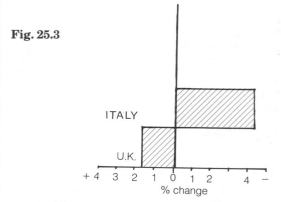

Country	Pop. 1980	1985	1990	% change 1980–1990
France	53.3	54.8	56.0	+5.1
Italy	61.3	59.6	58.6	−4.4
Belgium	9.8	9.8	9.9	+1.0
Ireland	3.3	3.5	3.7	+12.0
Spain	36.7	38.0	40.6	+10.6
Switzerland	6.3	6.3	6.3	0.0
United Kingdom	55.9	56.2	56.8	+1.6

Table 25.2

Unit 26

Movements of people inside countries

26.1 Introduction

People move from one town to another and from one region to another within the same country. These movements are called **internal migration**. These movements may be explained as being the results of what are called 'push and pull' factors. The 'push' factors encourage people to leave one place. The 'pull' factors are those which make certain areas attractive to people who live in other parts of the country.

Fig. 26.1 A model of 'push' factors

26.2 'Push' factors

The chief 'push' factors are shown in the cartoon below (Fig. 26.1).

You can see that people may be encouraged to move away both from country areas and cities. Most of the movement has been from the country to the towns. As a result, there have been many years of **rural depopulation**.

The most attractive parts of the cities to many people now are the suburbs. Many have moved from the inner city areas to the edges of the cities. The inner city areas have also become depopulated. Workers who once lived and worked there have found that old industries have closed down and there is no longer much work for them. So people have moved to new towns and estates on the edges of cities to find work. Many houses in the inner city are old. Some have been demolished. Many of the people who used to live in them have been re-housed elsewhere. This has increased the rate of migration from the inner city.

'PUSH FACTORS'

From rural areas   *From the inner city*

Poor uplands or backward farming techniques give low incomes.
Many people are poor

Poor quality houses

Farming is mechanised so there are fewer jobs on the farm

Old industries have closed down

Few job opportunities in the country areas for young people

Traffic congestion and pollution have made it less pleasant to live in the city centre

Bus and train services have declined. Petrol is more expensive. It is less convenient to live in the countryside

Redevelopment of the city centre has resulted in fewer homes there

Cottages in the country are bought up by outsiders and local people have to move away to get a home

People are afraid of increasing violence and crime

Farmers have been encouraged to give up small uneconomic farms

People may be moved to 'overspill' towns on the edge of the city

I lived on the family farm.
It could not keep us all

A

I used to be a farm labourer.
The hours were long
and the wages poor

B

I am staying with a cousin.
I am looking for a job.
there was no work at home

C

I lived in Algeria for 30 years
but had to come home when
it became independent

D

I wanted to be an actress
but have been working for
14 years as a waitress

E

I ran away from home
to come here.
I thought I would
make my fortune

F

26.3 'Pull' factors

The 'pull' factors are also very varied. The most powerful ones that attract people into the cities are:

1 The greater number of jobs that are available.

2 The wider range of jobs that exist in the city. Whereas in country towns and villages only a limited range of different types of job exists, in the cities there is a much wider choice. There is also a better chance of finding part-time jobs in the cities.

3 Wages are usually higher in shops, offices and works in the cities than they are in country towns and villages.

4 Parents believe that if they move to the city their children will have better opportunities for education and training.

5 Many migrants are attracted by the glamour of the city – famous sports teams to watch, entertainment, well-known shops and so on.

The suburbs also exert a 'pull' on many people because:

1 there is plenty of good quality housing;

2 it is more peaceful and leisurely than in the city centre;

Fig. 26.2

3 parents believe it is a good place in which to bring up children;

4 people can live near their work, for example, on new industrial estates;

5 it is often easy to get to motorways to travel.

Activities

A Fig. 26.2 shows six people who live in flats in an inner city area in Paris. All of them migrated from another area to Paris.

(a) Which two are examples of the process of rural depopulation?

(b) Which are in Paris because of the 'pull' of the large city?

(c) Which person is **not** an example of internal migration?

(d) Which two have not achieved what they hoped when they moved to Paris?

Activities continued

B Here are brief descriptions of five people who live in the same Paris suburb:

Man aged 50	– owns his own factory
Man aged 30	– a long distance lorry driver
Woman aged 28	– ex-school teacher with two young children
Woman aged 55	– used to live in a terraced house in the city centre which was demolished
Man aged 40	– builds houses

(a) Draw a diagram like Fig. 26.2 to illustrate this information.

(b) Which one of the five has been affected by a 'push' factor?

(c) For each of the others study the 'pull' of the suburbs opposite and then write a sentence to explain the factor which has probably attracted them to the suburb.

C Make a diagram like Fig. 26.1 to illustrate the 'pull' factors listed on the previous page. You will need to use a double page.

D Fig. 26.3 shows the chief population changes in Italy. The chief industrial towns of the country are Milan and Turin.

(a) Give one important reason why population has increased in the north-west of Italy.

(b) Suggest reasons why the population has increased in the region around Rome. Include at least one 'push' and one 'pull' factor.

(c) Find a relief map of Italy in your atlas. Suggest one reason why people may have left inland areas in central and southern Italy.

Fig. 26.3 Population changes in Italy

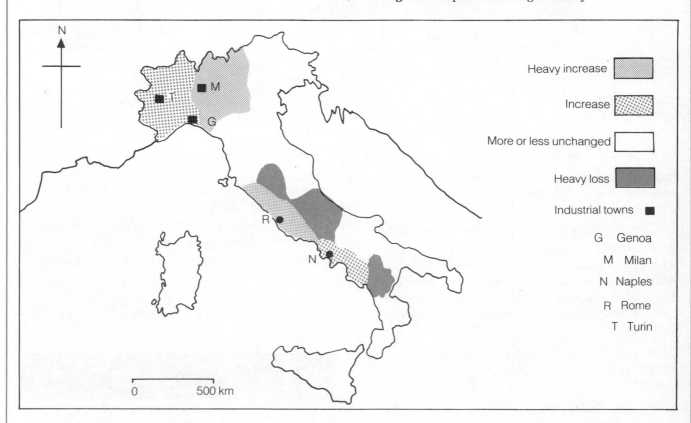

Legend:
- Heavy increase
- Increase
- More or less unchanged
- Heavy loss
- Industrial towns

G Genoa
M Milan
N Naples
R Rome
T Turin

0   500 km

Unit 27

Immigration

27.1 Introduction

Since the earliest times people have moved from one part of Europe to another. The present peoples of the British Isles for example, are the result of waves of invaders and refugees landing in Britain and mixing with those who already lived here. People who have moved away from their own countries are called **emigrants**. Those who have entered another country to live are called **immigrants**.

So an Englishman who goes to live in France is an emigrant from England and is an immigrant in France.

Fig. 27.1 The Berlin Wall

27.2 Causes of migration in Europe

The main reasons why people have migrated in modern times in Europe are:

1 War – millions of people left their homelands during the Second World War and many remained in the countries in which they found shelter.

2 Politics – since the Second World War many people have fled from the countries of Eastern Europe when these countries became communist. In particular East Germans escaped from the German Democratic Republic to the West (the Federal Republic). The photograph below shows the Berlin Wall which was built to stop escapes from East Berlin.

3 Economic – people have moved from poorer countries such as Turkey, Portugal and Yugoslavia to West Germany and Switzerland to find regular work. Many have settled with their families in the richer countries.

4 Retirement – wealthy people move from high tax countries to low tax countries such as Switzerland. Others follow the sun and buy retirement homes in Spain or Portugal where it is fairly cheap to live.

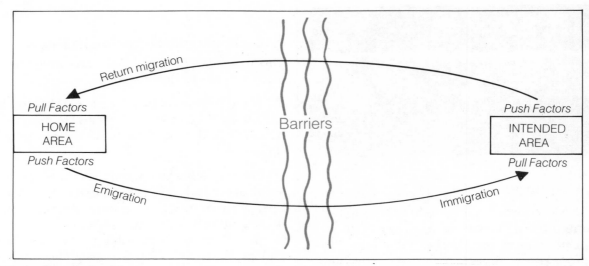

Fig. 27.2 A migration model

5 Religion – Jewish people have been persecuted in the USSR. Some have been allowed to leave Russia and have emigrated to Israel, or settled in western countries such as Sweden.

6 Natural disasters – in the last century many people left the Highlands of Scotland and Ireland when famine resulted from the failure of the potato harvest.

27.3 Illegal immigrants

Many people have wanted to move to the rich countries of Western Europe to live and work. But immigrants are only welcomed when there is a shortage of labour which affects the growth of industry and prosperity.

The rich countries limit the number of foreign workers they allow in. Some workers are so desperate that they try to enter countries illegally. Some immigrants are caught and refused entry or sent back to their own countries. When they do succeed some illegal immigrants get into debt because they had to pay high prices for false documents or for being smuggled in. They live in fear because if they are found out they may be sent back home.

Fig. 27.3
An immigrant
family

Activities

A Table 27.1 shows where immigrant workers came from to work in the Federal Republic of Germany (West Germany) in 1980.

Immigrant workers	Approximate totals
Total number of immigrant workers	1 950 000
Continent of origin:	
Africa	40 000
North and South America	28 000
Asia	75 000
Australia	2 500
Rest of Europe	1 800 000

Table 27.1

(a) Give two reasons why you think most foreign workers in the Federal Republic were from European countries rather than from other continents.

(b) Why do you think so few of the foreign workers in West Germany came from Australia?

(c) Name two Asian countries from which workers have emigrated to work in Western European countries.

(d) Draw bar graphs to represent the figures shown in the table above.

B The table opposite (Table 27.2) shows the countries from which the European foreign workers in the Federal Republic of Germany came in 1980.

Country of origin	Thousands
Austria	90
Greece	130
Italy	300
Portugal	60
Spain	85
Turkey	600
Yugoslavia	360
Others	175
Total	1800

Table 27.2

(a) Rearrange the countries in **descending** order of importance. Draw a bar graph to show the information for the countries in that order.

(b) Which of the causes of migration listed on the opposite page might account for the number of Yugoslav people who have gone to live and work in West Germany since the Second World War?

(c) Where are workers from Britain included in the table?

(d) Give two reasons why fewer workers from Britain have moved to West Germany to work than from other countries.

C Imagine that you are just about to leave school and that there is no hope of you finding a job in your home area. Would you be willing to go abroad to work?

List reasons for and against young people going to work abroad.

Unit 28

Rural depopulation

28.1 Introduction

Throughout the world people are drifting away from country areas and moving to the cities for the reasons discussed in Unit 26.

The most unattractive farming areas are the mountains and uplands in particular. Young people are not willing to put up with low standards of living which their parents and grandparents accepted. Rural depopulation is therefore a feature of most Western European countries. People have moved to large cities, industrial regions and along important routeways.

Upland areas are generally avoided by important routeways and, apart from mining centres, large commercial centres and administrative capitals are not often found in upland areas. So the more difficult areas of depopulation have become **zones of dispersal** of population.

28.2 The Massif Central of France

The Massif Central is a region in central southern France. It covers one-sixth of the area of France. The Massif is a highland area rising to 1866 metres above sea level. The climate is harsher than in the surrounding lowlands with more rainfall and many more frosts in the year. The soil is poor so the region does not favour arable farming.

As a result the region has long experienced rural depopulation. Whereas in the last 120 years the population of France has grown by 35 per cent, that of the Massif Central has fallen by 11 per cent. Outside the towns the fall has been 34 per cent.

The Massif is still chiefly a farming region. It has twice as big a proportion of people working on the land than the national average for France. It also has a larger proportion of elderly and a smaller proportion of young people than other regions of France. The value of the produce from Massif Central farms is less per hectare than in the Paris Basin to the north.

28.3 Fewer farmers

One of the major problems of the EEC (Common Market) was that so many farms in Europe were too small to provide a good living. In the Massif Central many farms were fragmented with one farmer owning land separated by fields owned by other farmers. To make the farms more profitable they needed to be larger and the land ownerships reorganized so that farms were not made up of separate bits. In twelve years about 90 000 farm holdings disappeared. Even so there are many small farms still, with nearly two-thirds less than twenty hectares in area.

Farmers have been offered special pensions to retire early. Young people have been given grants to leave farming and train for something else. So in recent years rural depopulation has been encouraged. But more prosperous farms, forestry, tourism and new industries may solve the region's problems.

Fig. 28.1

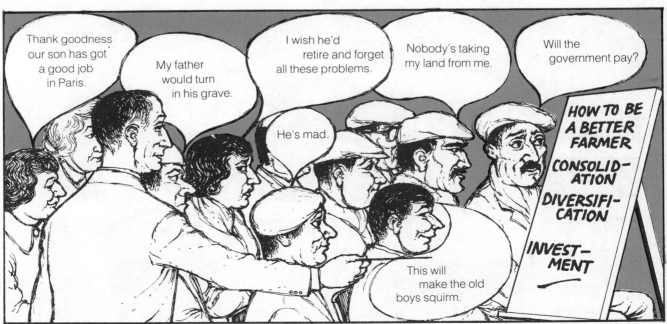

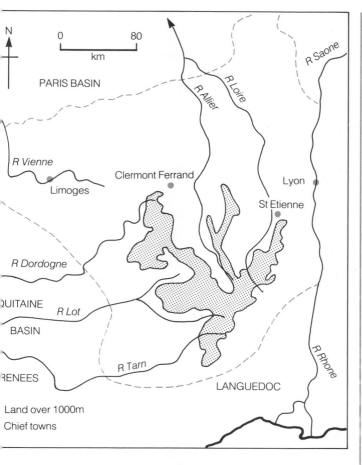

Fig. 28.2 The Massif Central

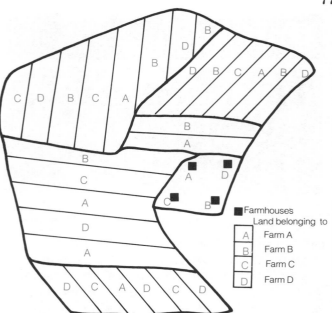

Fig. 28.3 Land ownership in a Massif Central village

(c) Make a tracing of the map. Change the ownership of the fields to make four consolidated farms. The French call consolidation 'remembrement'. If you wish you can even move the farmhouses.

(d) Explain the main advantages of the changes you have made.

B The changes which have been made in problem rural areas like the Massif Central were aimed at improving the lives of the people who live there. But there are also disadvantages which result from the changes and from the new economic activities. The table below shows some of the benefits and some of the costs of change.

Activities

A

Farmer	Age	Comments
A	59	My family have owned this land for 200 years
B	47	What do civil servants know about farming?
C	41	If I am going to stay here I need more land
D	52	The only thing I know is growing vines

Table 28.1

Fig. 28.3 shows a village in the south of France. The map shows who owns the land. In Table 28.1 you can see the ages of four farmers and the comments they have made about possible changes in farming in the village.

(a) Which of the four farmers is the happiest at the thought of reorganizing the ownership of land to consolidate (bring together) the farms?

(b) Which farmer will probably be the hardest to persuade that he should give up some of his own land to make better farm units?

Benefits (Advantages of change)	Costs (Disadvantages of change)
Farming is more efficient	Old ways of life disappear
Farmers who stay make a better living	Young people migrate to the cities
New industries bring better paid jobs	Lots of outsiders come to live there
Tourists spend money here	Country roads are clogged with tourist traffic
	House prices go up

Table 28.2

(a) Do the advantages outweigh the disadvantages? Give reasons for your answer.

(b) What do you think is the most important advantage? Why?

(c) What is the most serious disadvantage?

(d) Copy out the table as it is, and then add at least two advantages and two disadvantages to complete the table.

Unit 29

The functional regions of a city

29.1 Hamburg – a general introduction

Although Hamburg is 112 km up the estuary of the River Elbe it is an important north German port. As you can see from the map (Fig. 29.2) the River Elbe flows north-westwards from Czechoslovakia through the German Democratic Republic (East Germany) to reach Hamburg.

Before the Second World War (1939–1945) most of the trade which passed through Hamburg was with the towns and regions along the Elbe. After the division of Germany much of this trade was lost. A new canal link with the Ruhr and new motorways have enabled Hamburg to attract business from other West German regions.

Hamburg is also a very important industrial city. As you see below it has a free port into which goods can be brought duty free and processed and packed for export.

29.2 The functional regions of Hamburg

Hamburg is one of the chief cities of West Germany, and one of the richest. It has a large shopping centre with many famous shops and new shopping precincts. It is also a famous entertainment centre. There are twenty theatres, many cinemas, world famous opera and ballet, a casino and numerous night clubs and beer cellars. Its reputation as a lively city attracts many tourists.

The **Central Business District** (CBD) also contains some of the chief commercial offices in West Germany. When Germany was divided many important organizations in East Germany moved quickly to the West. The tobacco business moved from Dresden to Hamburg. Newsprint and book publishing firms also left Berlin and Leipzig for the city. Hamburg has now become an international exhibition centre with the German Boat Show and many clothing fairs held there.

The **free port** is a distinctive economic region of the city. Since goods can be handled duty free and processed for export, many industries have grown in the free port area. The most important is oil refining. Food processing such as the making of margarine and tea and coffee packing is also very important.

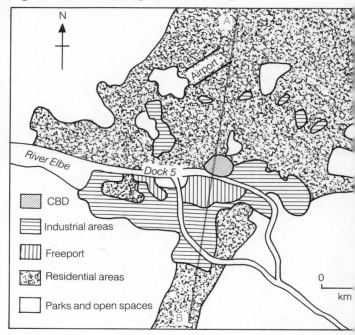

Fig. 29.1 Functional regions of Hamburg

- CBD
- Industrial areas
- Freeport
- Residential areas
- Parks and open spaces

Since it is a large port Hamburg has been able to build up **modern industries** which depend on imports. As you can see from the map the main industrial regions are located near the river and the docks. Important industries in the city are electrical engineering, shipbuilding, aluminium and aircraft manufacturing.

Hamburg was badly damaged during the war so parts of the city have been completely rebuilt. The prosperity of the city and the new industries have created the need for many **new homes**. The outer residential areas and suburbs have spread mainly northwards, since so many of the big industries are found in southern Hamburg.

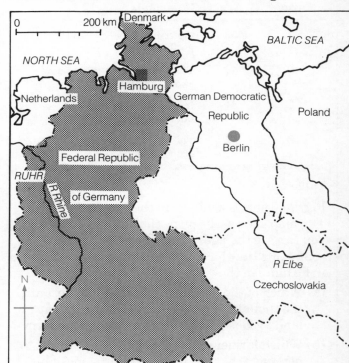

Fig. 29.2 The location of Hamburg

A   Hamburg

Fig. 29.3 Hamburg

B   Alster Lake

C   The fish market

D   The suburb of Blankensee

Activities

A The photographs in Fig. 29.3 show four scenes in the city of Hamburg. Study them and answer these questions.

(a) Which photograph shows part of the CBD?

(b) Which photograph shows an area located well away from the centre of the city?

(c) Which shows part of the free port area?

(d) From the evidence provided by photograph D describe the character of a residential area in Hamburg.

B Fig. 29.4 shows an urban transect (cross-section) of Hamburg along the line A B which is marked on Fig. 29.1. The portion of the transect from the River Elbe to point B has been completed to show the different types of activity that occur in particular areas to the south of the river.

(a) Complete the transect by naming functional regions A, B and C.

(b) What are the advantages of having the free port and industrial regions located next to each other?

(c) Name one advantage and one disadvantage of locating the airport on the edge of the city.

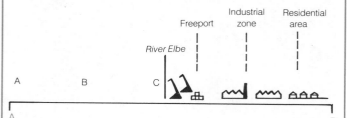

Fig. 29.4 A transect of the functional regions of Hamburg

Unit 30

Decay and redevelopment

30.1 Introduction

Most large cities in modern industrial countries share certain problems such as traffic congestion and the replacement of poor quality houses. In many cities these problems are the result of a lack of planning in the past.

30.2 Paris – a general introduction

Paris is an excellent example of a large city with many urban problems for which large scale programmes of redevelopment have been worked out and put into practice.

The Paris conurbation contains nearly 1 in 5 of all the people of France. The population of Greater Paris has grown rapidly for more than 150 years. Although the population of France as a whole fell in the first half of this century, that of Paris increased by more than 40 per cent. It is now more than 8 million.

30.3 Urban problems of Paris

The main problems which Paris has to face are:

1 overcrowding and the need to replace out of date houses;

2 traffic congestion in the city;

3 over-rapid growth in too short a time. The French say that 'the head (Paris) has grown too big for its body (France)';

4 the most modern industries concentrate around Paris. This makes the city even more of a magnet to people from other parts of France;

5 the growth of the city was not planned so the suburbs spread in an uncontrolled way.

30.4 Tackling the problems of Paris

A number of plans have been worked out and put into practice:

1 *Urban redevelopment schemes*
Older housing areas such as those in the Marais and Belleville districts have been modernized so that people can find decent homes inside the city. Old factories have been demolished. At Fronts de Seine tower blocks of flats and offices now stand where there used to be a car factory.

2 *New lines of transport have been built*
A new ring road, the Boulevard Périphérique, allows the motorist to avoid driving through Paris. The Regional Expressway is a new railway which runs right across Paris. The metro (underground) has also been extended to the suburbs.

3 *Factories and offices have moved away*
The government has encouraged factories and offices to move away from Paris to other French cities to make the capital less congested.

4 *A masterplan*
A masterplan for the future development of the Paris region has been put into practice. Eight new cities linked by motorways and express rail are to be built in two lines along the present Paris conurbation growth axes (Fig. 30.2).

Fig. 30.1
The east 'Périphérique' round Paris

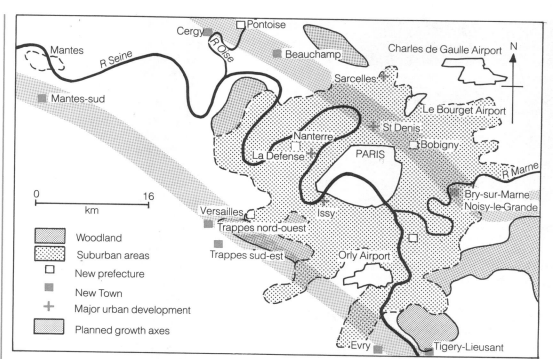

Fig. 30.2
The masterplan for Paris

Woodland
Suburban areas
☐ New prefecture
■ New Town
＋ Major urban development
Planned growth axes

Activities

A Above is the masterplan for Paris:

(a) Make a list of the eight new towns.

(b) Why do you think the new towns have been located well away from the new Charles de Gaulle airport?

(c) How many new towns are close to forest and woodland?

(d) What is the advantage of this to local residents?

(e) What disadvantages would you have to put up with if you lived in a new town such as Evry and worked in Paris?

B The photograph opposite shows part of the redevelopment of Paris. It is the Maine–Montparnasse scheme. On the site of an old railway station a new one has been built together with new offices and flats.

(a) What do we mean by 'urban redevelopment'?

(b) What is the advantage of building flats and offices next to the railway station?

(c) What are the disadvantages of living in a flat in Montparnasse?

C Table 30.1 compares ways in which Paris and London have tackled urban problems:

New features	London	Paris
Ring motorway	M25	
New underground	Jubilee and Victoria lines	
New towns (example)	Crawley	
Urban redevelopment scheme	Barbican	

Table 30.1

(a) Complete the table with reference to Paris.

(b) Explain why new transport schemes have been important for both cities.

(c) How does the building of new towns help to solve the cities' problems?

Fig. 30.3 The Maine-Montparnasse redevelopment scheme

Unit 31

The Central Business District

31.1 Introduction

In this section we shall look at the CBD of one of the most famous cities in Europe, Vienna, the capital of Austria.

31.2 Vienna – a general introduction

Today Vienna is the capital of a small neutral country with 7.5 million people. 20 per cent of the population of Austria live in Vienna itself so it is by far the most important city in Austria. In the early years of this century, however, it was the capital of the powerful Austro-Hungarian Empire.

Vienna then ruled Austria, Hungary, what is now Czechoslovakia, Northern Italy, Yugoslavia and part of Poland and Romania. Vienna was a city noted for wealth, music, food and fashion.

Although it is now far less important as a political centre it is still an international centre for music, tourism and fashion. The present CBD is made up mainly of the old city centre which was restored after the Second World War.

31.3 The CBD of Vienna

Fig. 31.1 is a tourist map of the CBD of Vienna. The boundary is more or less marked by a semi-circular road called the Ring.

This road was constructed on the site of the old city walls which were knocked down in 1857. New public buildings were built along it. The chief ones found on the Ring are marked on the map opposite (Fig. 31.2).

The centre of the CBD is the cathedral with the main shopping streets and restaurants nearby. Within the central area there are still many workshops and small factories. The city is world famous for luxury goods and clothing. Many of the workshops lie between the Stock Exchange and the Danube Canal.

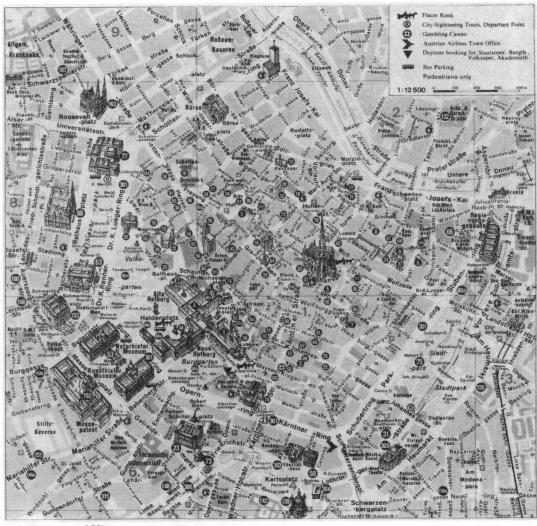

Fig. 31.1 A tourist map of Vienna

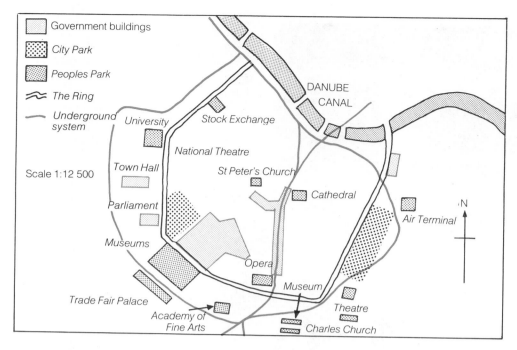

Fig. 31.2 Vienna: Central Business District

The houses in the CBD have many storeys (floors). Some have become offices and business premises. There are many embassies in Vienna, some of which are in mansions around the edges of the Ring.

Vienna is an expensive city, noted for the quality of the services it offers. Many international fashion houses show their collections there and the clothes shops are found alongside antique shops, art galleries and jewellers.

Vienna's CBD is therefore a national and international centre as well as being the core of the city.

The table below shows the main problems and the solutions to date:

Problems
1 Old city has narrow winding roads
2 Main railway stations are not near the CBD
3 The tram system around the Ring takes up a great deal of land
4 As suburbs grow more people must commute
5 The airport is on the edge of the city
6 International tourists overcrowd the CBD in summer
7 Bridges cause bottlenecks

Solutions so far
1 New metro (underground) system has been built
2 Main shopping streets turned into a pedestrian precinct
3 An air terminal has been placed near the city centre by the City Park

Table 31.1

(a) Which of the problems listed have been eased by the building of the metro?

(b) List the advantages of the pedestrian shopping streets or other ways of separating pedestrians and traffic.

(c) What are the disadvantages for the shopkeepers if cars and lorries cannot go down shopping streets?

(d) Look at Fig. 31.2. Has the air terminal been well placed? Give reasons.

(e) The tram system is slow but it is cheap and reliable. What advantages would there be in removing it?

(f) Why is the Ring tram system especially popular with the tourists?

Activities

A Look at the map of the CBD above and the tourist map opposite. Then on the tourist map:

(a) Find the Ring.
(b) Find the Royal Palace and the City Park which are alongside the Ring.
(c) Find the Stock Exchange.

B **(a)** Draw a transect of the CBD from south-west to north-east to show as many characteristic features as possible of the CBD of Vienna.

(b) Label your transect.
(c) Write short notes on what it shows.

C Like the centre of all big cities the CBD of Vienna suffers from traffic congestion.

Unit 32

A hierarchy of towns

Towns which belong to the lower ranks carry out tasks for the people who live in the local area. Large towns and cities of high rank carry out services for many more people who are attracted from a much wider area.

The lower rank towns have shops which sell day-to-day goods. The high rank centres have large and well-known shops which people travel many kilometres to visit.

Fig. 32.1

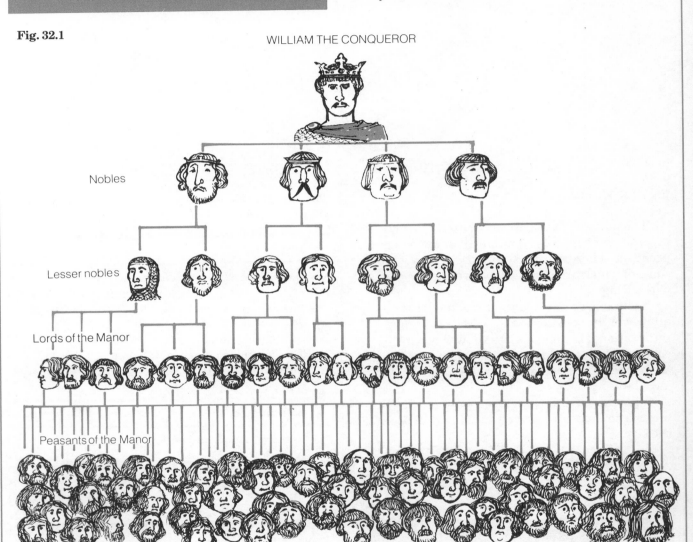

WILLIAM THE CONQUEROR

Nobles

Lesser nobles

Lords of the Manor

Peasants of the Manor

32.1 What is a hierarchy?

A hierarchy is a pattern of organization in which parts belong to different grades. Above is a hierarchy you will have heard of in history. It is the feudal system by which people were classed in the time of the Normans. You can see that from the King downwards different groups of people were graded into different levels of society.

32.2 The urban hierarchy

Towns and cities also relate to each other in the form of a hierarchy.

Towns are grouped into different grades or ranks according to their size and importance.

32.3 The urban hierarchy in the Frankfurt region

Fig. 32.2 shows the hierarchy of towns in the Frankfurt area of the Federal Republic of Germany. The chief city is Frankfurt itself.

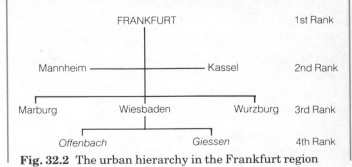

FRANKFURT		1st Rank
Mannheim ——————————— Kassel		2nd Rank
Marburg Wiesbaden Wurzburg		3rd Rank
Offenbach *Giessen*		4th Rank

Fig. 32.2 The urban hierarchy in the Frankfurt region

Frankfurt is so important that many talk of the city as the 'hidden' capital of West Germany. It is the financial centre of the country and many firms have their headquarters in the city. It is also a rich industrial city.

The examples in the second rank, Mannheim and Kassel are also important towns but are not as big or as powerful as Frankfurt. Mannheim for example is a port on the Rhine with oil refineries, a nuclear power station, chemical works and a lorry factory. It also has a very modern shopping centre.

Many of the smaller towns such as Würzburg grew up as market centres for rich farming areas. The smallest towns such as Giessen have picturesque local shopping centres.

32.4 The urban hierarchy of West Germany

Fig. 32.3 (a) and (b) show the pattern for the country as a whole. The four chief centres are Frankfurt, Munich, Cologne and Hamburg. They act as the main service centres for large parts of the country (Fig. 32.3(a)). Fig. 32.3(b) shows the towns of the four main ranks (grades) in the urban hierarchy.

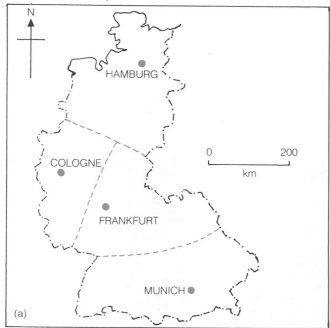

(a)

Activities

A (a) Look again at the hierarchy shown in Fig. 32.1. Work out the pattern of the hierarchy in your school. You do not need to draw 'portraits'! Here is a start:

Headteacher
|
Deputy Head
|

(b) What town in your area would you go to if you wanted to:

  (i) buy some food in a supermarket;

 (ii) look around Marks & Spencer;

(iii) buy clothes in a big departmental store;

 (iv) visit a famous shop that attracts people from a very wide area?

If you name the same place for all four you probably live in or near a large city. Most people will name more than one place.

(c) From your answers work out a hierarchy of shopping centres which you and your family use.

B Table 32.1 gives the approximate population of eight towns and cities in the Frankfurt region.

City	Population	Rank
Frankfurt	630 000	
Giessen	75 000	
Kassel	200 000	
Mannheim	300 000	
Marburg	75 000	
Offenbach	100 000	
Wiesbaden	275 000	
Wurzbürg	125 000	

Table 32.1

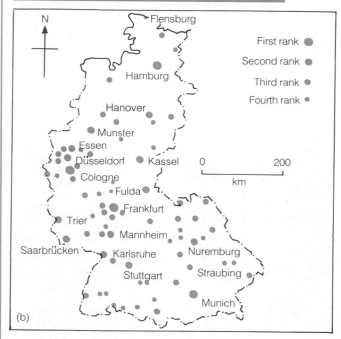

(b)

Fig. 32.3 (a) and (b)

(a) Look back to Fig. 32.2. Use it to complete the 'rank' column in the table.

(b) Draw a figure like 32.2 but instead of the names of the towns put in the population figures.

(c) Is there a perfect match between population size and rank? What are the exceptions, if any, to the broad pattern?

Transport

Unit 33

Road networks

33.1 The Autostrada del Sole

The photograph shows one of the most important routeways in Italy. It is the Autostrada del Sole (Sunshine motorway) which runs from Milan in the north to Reggio in the 'toe' of Italy, a distance of 1250 kilometres.

Italy has nearly 6000 kilometres of motorway with the densest network in the north where there are 3900 km. The building of a good network of roads has been very important in Italy because the shape of the country results in long distances between the north and the south.

The southern half of the peninsula and the islands of Sicily and Sardinia are very much poorer than the north (see Fig. 33.2). This contrast between north and south has been brought about because the south (known as the Mezzogiorno) is mainly a neglected agricultural region whereas the north is a prosperous industrial and agricultural region. Lack of jobs and rural poverty forced 4 million people to leave the Mezzogiorno between 1951 and 1971.

In 1950 the Cassa per il Mezzogiorno (Fund for the South) was set up by the government and a number of schemes were started to improve conditions. At first changes were made to agriculture and then in the 1960s money was spent developing industry.

In addition motorways were built to open up the region with the Autostrada del Sole as the main link between Milan and Naples. South of Rome the route of the motorway was deliberately planned to run through some of the poorest rural areas.

The Autostrada del Sole has made it possible for goods produced in Naples to reach Milan in eight hours. Extensions to the motorway network south of Naples allow traffic to travel the length of the peninsula in less than a day. Fig. 33.2 opposite shows the Autostrada del Sole and the rest of the motorway network in Italy.

Fig. 33.1 Autostrada del Sole, Italy

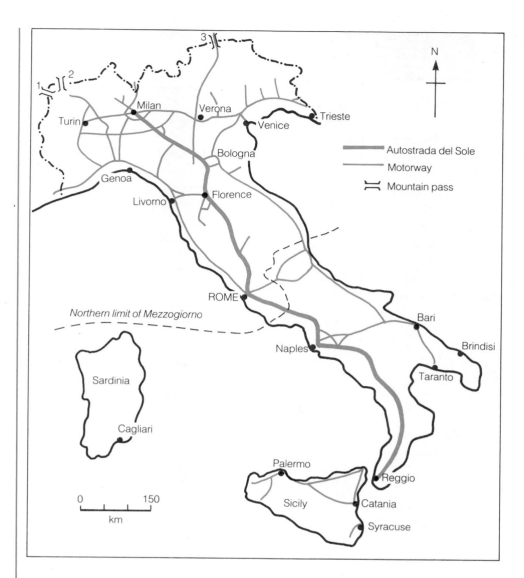

Fig. 33.2 The Italian motorway network

Legend:
- Autostrada del Sole
- Motorway
- ⨝ Mountain pass

33.2 How the motorway has helped the Mezzogiorno

1 One of the problems of the south before the motorway was built was its isolation. Improvements to farming made by the Cassa per il Mezzogiorno meant that markets were needed for the increased output from the farms. The motorway made it possible to grow fresh fruit and vegetables in the south and sell them in the industrial cities of the north such as Milan, Turin and Genoa. Wine, fruit, tomatoes, sugar and other farm crops travel along the motorway to these markets in the north, or to other countries, such as Britain, which also belong to the EEC. Some of the farm products are processed in new factories in the south and travel in cans and packages. Trucks from the north carry surplus farm products such as rice, as well as manufactured goods, to the south.

2 Money spent in the south on new factories has helped to reduce unemployment and bring new life to the region. These factories have been built close to the motorways with concentrations around Naples, further south in the 'heel' of Italy, and in eastern Sicily. Large firms with factories in the north have been encouraged to build new plants in the south. As a result one of the largest car manufacturers, Fiat, has built a car plant near Naples making some of the parts there, and using engines and other components brought by truck from its factory in Turin. Olivetti, which makes typewriters and computers in the north, has also built factories in the Naples area.

3 In recent years the Mezzogiorno has started to develop a tourist industry. The motorways have opened up the countryside and coastline and the region is attracting an increasing number of visitors from northern and western Europe. The south has many historic sites, attractive beaches and a great deal of sunshine to attract tourists from the north. The motorway network is helping to develop the Mezzogiorno although there is still a gap between the standard of living in the north and south of Italy, and it is still the poorest region in western Europe.

Activities

A Answer the following questions about Fig. 33.2.

(a) What are the names of the three mountain passes numbered 1, 2 and 3 on the map?
(b) With which countries do they link Italy?

(c) Approximately how far is it in a straight line from Turin to Taranto? Compare your answer with the distance from London to Edinburgh.

B Draw an outline of Italy south of Rome and add the towns and motorways shown on Fig. 33.2. Show the following industrial development by placing suitable symbols near the names of the towns.

cars – Naples, Bari; aircraft – Naples; engineering – Augusta; office machinery – Naples; oil refining – Augusta, Taranto, Bari, Cagliari; petro-chemicals – Brindisi, Augusta, Naples; steel – Taranto, Naples; textiles – Naples.

C

Year	Agriculture	Industry	Services
1950	57	20	23
1970	33	32	35
1980	25	35	40

Table 33.1 Employment by percentage in the Mezzogiorno

Fig. 33.3 shows employment in 1950 as a horizontal bar graph.

(a) Draw horizontal bar graphs to show the 1970 and 1980 employment percentages. To make the graphs you must:

  (i) Draw a scale line to represent 100% (a line 10 cm long for example).

  (ii) Draw rectangles the same lengths as the scale line.

  (iii) Divide the first rectangle into the percentages required, making sure that the highest percentage is on the left, then the next highest and so on. Mark the second bar in the same order as the first (even though this may mean that the highest percentage is not on the left).

  (iv) Shade or colour in each section of the bars.

  (v) Give your chart a key and title.

D Use a road atlas to follow the route taken by a truck carrying Olivetti typewriters from the factory at Caserta north of Naples to London. Use the motorway network whenever possible. Make a list of the countries and main cities the truck would pass through. Note the countries which belong to the EEC.

E Design an advertisement to encourage business people to move their firms to the Mezzogiorno.

Fig. 33.3 The Mezzogiorno-percentages in the main types of employment, 1950

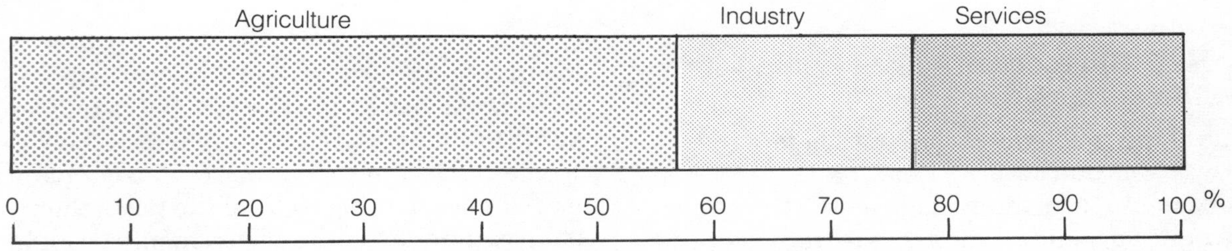

Unit 34

Rail networks

34.1 French Railways – the TGV

The TGV train (Train à Grande Vitesse) in the photograph gives part of France the fastest train service in the world. The TGV holds the world rail speed record of 379 km/h (236 mph). To make this possible the French have built a specially designed track from Paris to Lyon, a distance of 426 kilometres. On this track the TGV can keep up a steady speed of 260 km/h (160 mph).

The new service has cut the travelling time from Paris to Lyon from 3 hours 50 minutes to 2 hours. Times to other cities on the same network have also been cut drastically, although the highest speeds can only be reached on the length of specially constructed track. Nevertheless, Marseille is now less than 5 hours by rail from Paris.

34.2 Reasons for introducing the TGV

France has the busiest railway network in Europe outside the USSR and, as Fig. 34.2 on the next page shows, the busiest section of that network is the line from Paris to Lyon and Marseille. Much of this routeway follows the valley of the River Rhône or its tributary the River Saône. It is called the Rhône-Saône corridor and is one of the most important routeways in Europe, linking the Mediterranean with the countries of Europe which border the North Sea. Paris, Marseille and Lyon are the three largest cities in France and there is a great deal of movement of goods and people from one to the other.

In recent years French railways have suffered from competition from the airlines and the only way the service could fight back was by developing faster trains. The new line and the high-speed trains designed for it have given work to many French firms, particularly engineering factories and steel producers. The French hope that orders for similar high-speed trains will come from other countries to provide more work for industry.

34.3 The significance of the TGV

Since the TGV service was started in 1981 many passengers have switched from the airlines to trains. A survey found that nearly 2 out of 5 first-class passengers travelling from Paris to Lyon on the TGV would have taken a flight rather than use a normal train.

Business in both Paris and Lyon has benefited from the new service. Lyon is the most important city between Paris and Marseille and its position on the Rhône-Saône corridor gives it links with Switzerland and Italy. It is the regional capital for the surrounding towns and countryside and the centre for many industries.

Not everyone was happy when the new line was built. Some people considered that it should have been built to one of the poorer regions of France to the west or south-west of Paris. Instead it was built in the already prosperous eastern side of the country.

Fig. 34.1 TGV train

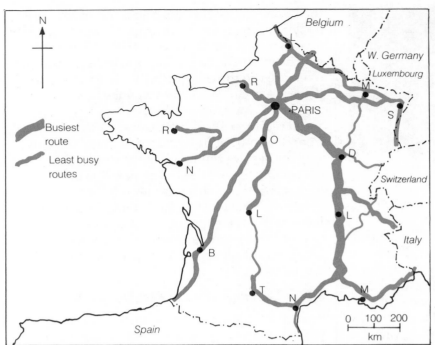

Fig. 34.2 The busiest and least busy routes on French railways

It has now been agreed that a new line will be built to link Paris with the south-west and this will mean work for at least 4000 people. When it is finished Bordeaux will be less than 3 hours from Paris by rail. Some people believe that the next high-speed service should link Paris with Brussels and Amsterdam, or with Germany. Crossing these international frontiers does, however, present some problems unless the neighbouring countries agree to use the French system. It is unlikely that West Germany would do this because it is experimenting with a different type of train which 'floats' above a central guide rail and is known as the Transrapid. When new track has been built for this train it will travel even faster than the TGV.

Activities

A Look at Fig. 34.2 which shows the busiest routes on French Railways. The least busy routes on the network are also shown.

(a) Which parts of the network are the busiest, those to the east or those to the west of Paris?

(b) Which one of the following is the best description of the network:
 (i) circular, linking cities around the edge of the country;
 (ii) radial, like the spokes of a wheel;
 (iii) linear, with branches like a tree?

B Use Fig. 34.2 to draw a network diagram of the French Railway network. Use an atlas to find the names of the cities shown by their first letter. Add the names to the network. Fig. 34.3 shows a more detailed section of the network.

C The table below shows the number of trains from Paris each Wednesday using the part of the

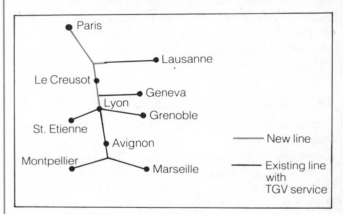

Fig. 34.3 Part of the TGV network

railway network shown in Fig. 34.3. The departure and arrival times of the fastest services are also given.

Route	No.	Dept.	Arr.
Paris – Lyon – St Etienne	3	13.00	15.48
Paris – Geneva	4	07.35	11.06
Paris – Lyon – Grenoble	3	06.45	09.57
Paris – Lausanne	4	12.28	16.10
Paris – Marseille	10	10.28	15.08
Paris – Montpellier	6	15.40	20.25

Table 34.1 TGV trains from Paris each Wednesday using the network shown in Fig. 34.3

(a) How long does the journey take from Paris to
 (i) St Etienne; **(ii)** Geneva; **(iii)** Grenoble;
(iv) Lausanne; **(v)** Marseille; **(vi)** Montpellier?

(b) How many TGV trains from Paris pass through the following cities each Wednesday?
 (i) Le Creusot; **(ii)** Lyon; **(iii)** Avignon.

Unit 35

Airports

35.1 The busiest airports

London airport (Heathrow, Gatwick and Stansted) is the busiest airport in Europe, followed by Paris (Orly and Charles de Gaulle), Frankfurt and the other cities shown on Fig. 35.1.

There are two main types of flights at airports. International flights travel to and from other countries while domestic flights are between cities in the same country. Nearly all the passengers who pass through Amsterdam's airport are on international flights, whereas nearly half the passengers at Munich are on domestic flights. All the airports shown on the map owe most of their importance to their international flights. London (Heathrow), for example, is the busiest international airport in the world with 84 per cent of its passengers booked on international flights.

Fig. 35.1 Europe's ten busiest airports

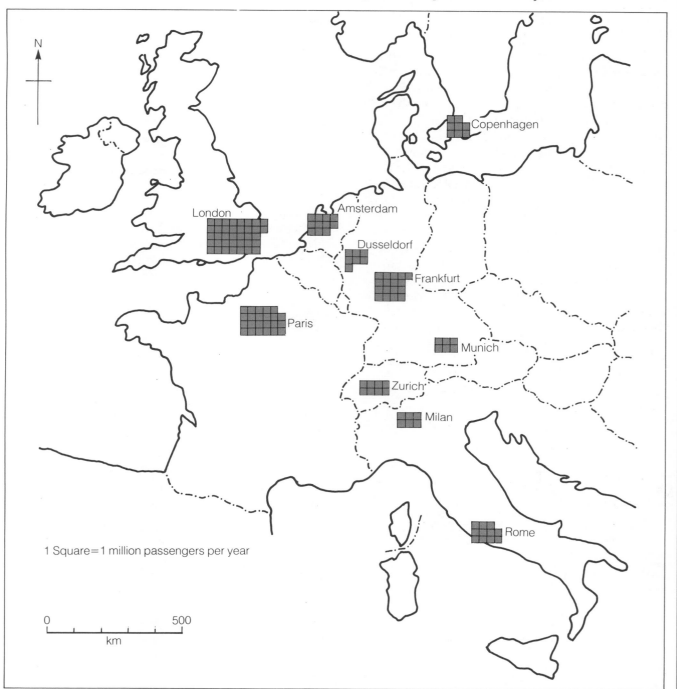

1 Square = 1 million passengers per year

0   500

km

Fig. 35.2 Frankfurt airport

35.2 The siting of large airports

In Book 1, Unit 38, you may have read about the factors which help to decide where an airport is built. Fig. 35.3 below shows the position of Frankfurt-am-Main airport, the busiest airport in West Germany. The capital city, Bonn, is small with no large industries and Frankfurt has developed as the country's leading airport.

Many of the cities shown on Fig. 35.1 have built airports in recent years to replace others which were too small to cope with large modern aircraft and the increase in traffic. Modern international airports need much land and have to be built some way from the city centres. For example, the Charles de Gaulle airport at Paris covers 3000 hectares and is 23 kilometres from the city centre. The old airport (Le Bourget), which is now closed, was only 10 kilometres from the heart of Paris and was very much smaller.

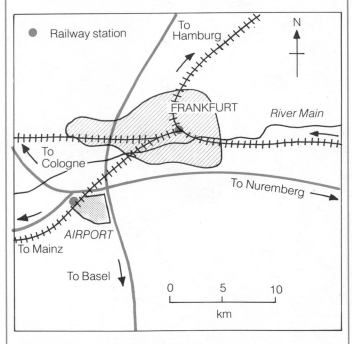

Fig. 35.3 The position of Frankfurt airport

Activities

A (a) Make a list of the airports shown in Fig. 35.1 in order of importance, with the busiest airport at the top of your list.

(b) Write down the capital cities on the map which also have busy airports.

(c) Discuss why most capital cities in Europe have busy airports.

B (a) Use the table below to find the average distance of the ten airports from the city centre.

Airport	Distance from city centre (km)
Amsterdam	15
Copenhagen	10
Düsseldorf	11
Frankfurt	15
London (Heathrow)	24
Milan	8
Munich	10
Paris (C. de G.)	23
Rome	30
Zurich	11

Table 35.1

(b) Copenhagen airport is close to the city's suburbs and 10 km from the city centre. A new airport is planned on the island of Saltholm 20 km from the city centre. The island would be linked to the city by a bridge. Discuss how the following people might feel about the new development.

(i) Someone living close to the present airport

(ii) A businessman working in the city centre who uses the airport regularly

(iii) A farmer living on the island of Saltholm

C Use your atlas and Fig. 35.1 to make a list of reasons why Frankfurt is the most important airport in West Germany.

D Frankfurt has domestic services to a number of important cities in West Germany. There are the following number of flights from Frankfurt each Wednesday:

Bayreuth 3; West Berlin 15; Bremen 4; Düsseldorf 10; Cologne 8; Hamburg 13; Hanover 6; Munich 16; Munster 4; Nuremberg 5; Saarbrucken 4; Stuttgart 4.

(a) Trace a map of West Germany and mark on it Frankfurt and the twelve cities in the list above.

(b) Draw lines from Frankfurt to each of the cities with the thickness of the lines indicating the density of the flights. Put a scale for the flight numbers in your key.

Unit 36

Air networks

36.1 Air travel

Travelling by air has become an important way of getting about Europe. There are two main types of air travellers, business people and tourists.

The most regular air travellers are business people who must attend meetings, talk to customers and see other businesses and factories for themselves. For these people time is money. An Amsterdam businessman with a meeting in Paris can fly there and back in a morning. The train journey takes 5½ hours and the businessman would be away from his office for at least a day if he travelled by train.

The second group of air travellers is tourists. They travel by air to reach their holiday destination quickly and conveniently. Unlike business travel, the tourist trade is seasonal with peaks at weekends and during the holiday seasons of June to August, Christmas and Easter. The main tourist routes in western Europe are north – south, from the cooler climates of the north to the sunshine and warmth of the Mediterranean. In winter routes to the ski resorts in Switzerland, Austria and France are also very busy.

A third group of air travellers has a variety of reasons for travelling. They include visiting relatives or friends, attending special events such as football matches and going to hospitals for special treatment.

Freight is also carried by aircraft. Some flights carry only freight but much is taken by the regular passenger services. Sending goods by air is expensive when compared with other forms of transport but aircraft have the advantage of speed. Goods best sent by air are those of high value and little weight, e.g. diamonds, watches; and those which are fragile or perishable, e.g. scientific instruments and early strawberries.

36.2 European air networks

Nearly all European countries have their own airlines. Exceptions are the countries of Norway, Denmark and Sweden which have set up a joint airline called SAS (Scandinavian Airlines System). Fig. 36.2 shows the network of routes inside Sweden. Some parts of this network are

Fig. 36.1 An SAS Tristar

served by small private airlines and not by SAS. The areas with a low density of population have few air links whereas those regions and towns in Sweden where most people live have regular domestic air services.

A busy route is best measured by the number of passengers who use it, rather than the number of aircraft which fly along it. There is a number of

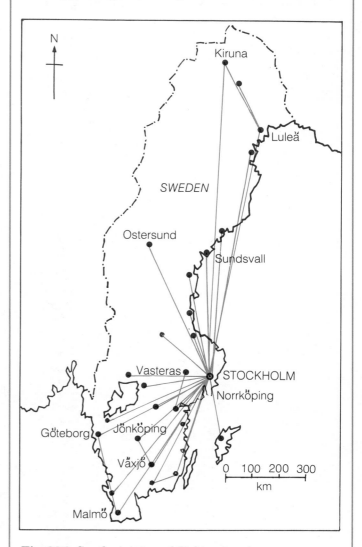

Fig. 36.2 Sweden's internal flight network

reasons why some air routes are busier than others. A European route is likely to carry large numbers of passengers if:

(a) the settlements at either end are large, e.g. the route from Paris to Marseille is busier than that from Paris to Toulon;

(b) the route crosses water, e.g. London to Paris, Oslo to Copenhagen;

(c) there is much trade between the regions at either end of the route, e.g. Cologne and Rotterdam;

(d) the route is used by tourists, e.g. London to Malaga in Spain.

Activities

A Look at Fig. 36.2

(a) Which city is at the centre of the network?

(b) Which is the closest city to Stockholm to have a direct air link with the capital?

(c) Approximately how far is it from the city in (b), to Stockholm?

(d) By which two routes can people living in Malmö fly to Kiruna?

(e) Which cities are served by direct flights from Jönköping?

B Make a copy of the outline of Sweden on Fig. 36.2

(a) Shade in one large area where you would expect to find a low density of population.

(b) Shade in one large area where you would expect to find a high density of population.

(c) Add a key and title to your map.

C Look at Fig. 36.3 which shows the air links between Norway, Denmark, Sweden and Finland.

(a) What are the names of the four capital cities shown on the map?

(b) Which capital city has the largest number of links with other Scandinavian countries?

(c) Which capital city has the smallest number of links with other cities?

(d) Why does Malmö in southern Sweden have a busy air link with Copenhagen which is only 20 kilometres away?

D Write down the following names of European airlines and against each one put the country of origin.

Swissair; Sabena; Aeroflot; KLM; Lufthansa; Finnair; Alitalia; TAP; LOT; Iberia.

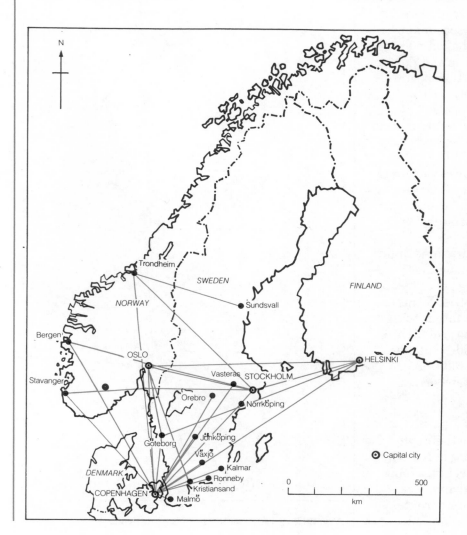

Fig. 36.3 Regular air services between the Scandinavian countries

Unit 37

Inland waterways

37.1 Moving goods by water

Canals in Europe which are used to carry goods are much wider and deeper than those in Britain. The barges are also different. They are very large and usually self-propelled. **Push-barge convoys** are also common. These consist of a number of barges without engines which are joined together and then pushed along by a powerful pusher vessel. These push-barge convoys operate on the navigable rivers which form the largest and most important part of the network of European waterways. This network is at its densest in the Netherlands where one-third of all the goods transported travel by water.

Water transport is much slower than rail or road. It takes over a week to make the journey of nearly 1000 km up the Rhine from Rotterdam to Basel. However, the cost per tonne for each kilometre is lower than by road or rail and considerable improvements have been made to the waterway network to make it competitive with the other forms of transport.

Fig. 37.1 Major waterways in Europe

37.2 The Rhine waterway

The River Rhine and its tributaries is by far the most important waterway in Europe. It carries four times as much as all the other waterways combined and is a busy routeway between the North Sea and central Europe. Coal is no longer as important a cargo on the Rhine as it used to be. The main materials moving upstream from Rotterdam are iron ore and oil products for the Ruhr industrial region. Downstream the most important cargoes are of sand and gravel, iron and steel products and coal.

Along the Rhine have grown the river ports of Duisburg, Cologne, Mannheim, Strasbourg and Basel.

Activities

A **(a)** Make a copy of Fig. 37.1 and use your atlas to help you
 (i) name the countries shown on the map;
 (ii) name the waterways which are numbered 1–15. Here is a list of their names:
   Kiel Canal; Elbe; Weser; Dortmund-Ems Canal; Mittelland Canal; North Sea Canal; Albert Canal; Seine, Rhône-Saône; Moselle; Rhine; Main; Danube; Neckar; Po.

(b) Add dotted lines to your map to show two new or improved waterway links which should be developed to take barges of 1350 tonnes or more.

(c) Give reasons why these new waterways should be built.

B The following table shows the amount of tonnage handled by the major inland ports of the European waterway network.

Inland port	Tonnage handled 1983 (million tonnes)
Amsterdam	23.3
Basel	8.0
Cologne	12.0
Duisburg	20.5
Frankfurt	10.2
Ghent	5.8
Liège	13.6
Mannheim	8.6
Paris	19.3
Strasbourg	11.7

Table 37.1

Show the information from Table 37.1 on your map of the inland waterways of Europe. Use a scale of 1 sq mm = 5 million tonnes. Make your squares with 2 mm sides (see Fig. 35.1).

Country	Road	Rail	Inland waterway	Pipeline
Belgium	13.7	61.8	18.3	6.2
France	12.5	77.0	5.1	5.4
W Germany	9.7	80.2	7.8	2.3
Italy	11.3	82.0	0.1	6.6
Netherlands	2.8	57.7	34.1	5.4
UK	10.0	86.7	0.3	3.0

Table 37.2 The relative importance of the different forms of transport used for goods, 1982 (per cent)

C **(a)** Suggest reasons why inland waterways play an important part in the transport of goods in the Netherlands and not in Britain.

(b) What kinds of raw materials are carried long distances by pipelines?

(c) What major form of transport is not included on Table 37.2?

(d) Why do you think this form of transport does not appear?

(e) What kinds of goods are best carried by this form of transport?

Unit 38

Coastal ports

38.1 Rotterdam

Rotterdam is the busiest port in the world and it owes its importance to its position at the mouth of the River Rhine and on improvements made to the harbour and its approaches. Rotterdam handles over 250 million tonnes of cargo each year, four-fifths of this cargo being unloaded from sea-going vessels.

The small medieval harbour was some 30 kilometres from the open sea and could only be approached along a winding channel. This channel was deepened and straightened in 1872 to form the New Waterway which made it possible for large ships to reach the docks which had developed along the left bank of the river.

During the Second World War Rotterdam was very badly damaged and the city and its docks had to be rebuilt when the war ended. The first major extension downstream was on marshland which was drained to form Europoort, a harbour area to deal with the large bulk-carriers and supertankers bringing raw materials and oil to the industrial areas of the European Economic Community.

In recent years there have been further extensions to the harbour. To provide space for new industries a new island, called Maasvlakte, has been made by reclaiming land from the sea. On the right bank a new container port, called Rijnpoort, has been built by cutting docks out of the soft marshland.

Rotterdam is an **entrepôt** port. This means that it deals mainly with the distribution of goods to other places by transferring them from ocean-going ships to barges, or vice-versa. Like most ports it has developed industries, based on the needs of the shipping which uses the port, and on incoming raw materials. The city's industries include shipbuilding and repairing, oil refining, flour milling and chemical processing.

Fig. 38.1 Part of the port of Rotterdam

Activities

A The ports shown on Fig. 38.2 are listed in Table 38.1 below.

Port	Tonnage handled 1983 (million tonnes)
Antwerp	84.1
Barcelona	18.4
Bergen	11.5
Bilbao	24.0
Bordeaux	10.5
Gdansk	12.8
Göteborg	22.7
Hamburg	61.9
Le Havre	58.1
Lisbon	13.1
Marseille	91.6
Narvik	18.0
Rostock	15.7
Rotterdam	252.4
Wilhelmshaven	25.6

Table 38.1 The tonnage handled by the major continental ports of Europe, 1983

(a) Make a copy of the map and show the ports according to their size using the key shown in Fig. 38.4. Add the names of the ports and a key to your map.

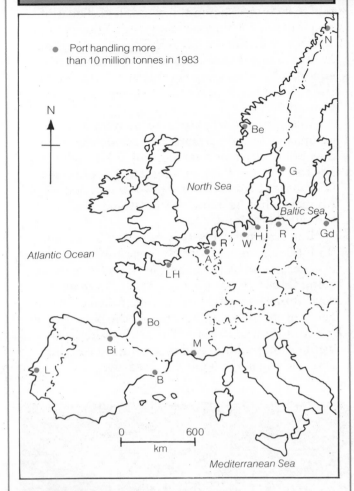

Fig. 38.2 Major continental sea ports in Europe

Fig. 38.4 Symbols to be used in Activity A

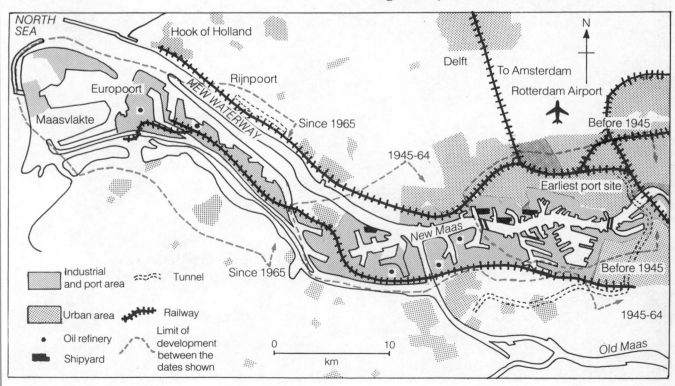

Fig 38.3 The growth and development of Rotterdam

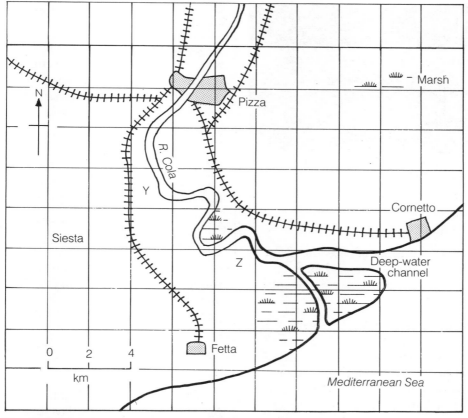

Fig. 38.5 Planning map for the development of Pizza as a port

(b) Which countries have the four largest ports?
(c) For which country is Gdansk the port?
(d) What is the total tonnage handled by the ports in West Germany?

B Look at Fig. 38.3.

(a) Why are there no oil refineries near the older docks at Rotterdam?
(b) What advantages has Rijnpoort as a container port?
(c) What port industries would you expect to develop at Maasvlakte?

C The government of Siesta, an EEC country in the south of Europe, is anxious to develop its port at Pizza as a major Common Market port on the Mediterranean. Imagine you are one of the planners called in to advise the government and that you have just returned from studying the developments at Rotterdam.

(a) Make a copy of Fig. 38.5 using squared paper and mark on it your recommendations for:
  (i) the channel of the River Cola between Y and Z;
 (ii) the site for an oil refinery taking up 6 sq km of land;
(iii) the site for a container terminal (2 sq km);
 (iv) an industrial site (4 sq km);
  (v) the site for shipbuilding and repair yards (2 sq km).

(b) List your reasons for each of the recommendations you have made.

Unit 39

Transport in cities

39.1 Traffic problems

Traffic causes problems in nearly all European cities and there are several reasons why these problems occur.

1 In recent years the number of cars and other vehicles using the roads has increased very rapidly, particularly in cities where most people live.

2 Many European cities have become very much larger as people have been attracted to live in them and work in factories and service industries. City centres have become congested with more people crowding into them to work and more firms looking for office space in the Central Business District.

3 Most European cities have developed gradually over many hundreds of years. The oldest part, around which the city grew up, often dates back to the Middle Ages or earlier. The streets are narrow and quite unsuitable for vehicles or crowds of pedestrians.

4 Cities are centres of communication networks with important routes meeting in the centre. Unless new roads are built, through traffic on busy routes can seriously add to the congestion, causing traffic jams on major roads.

39.2 Solving the problems

One example of a city which has tried to solve its traffic problems is Brussels, the capital of Belgium. The city grew up along the valley of the small River Senne with the old centre forming a five-sided shape (pentagon), surrounded by wide boulevards. This is now the chief commercial and shopping district of the city with narrow streets and many old historic buildings. Some government offices are on higher ground overlooking the old city.

Brussels is the headquarters of the EEC whose main building is about 2 kilometres from the city centre.

On the edge of the city are the headquarters of NATO (North Atlantic Treaty Organization). These large organizations, together with the Belgian government, employ many thousands of typists, clerks and other service workers. As a result, three out of every four people who work in Brussels are employed in the service industries.

Fig. 39.1 Traffic in Brussels

Fig. 39.2 N.A.T.O. Headquarters, Brussels

The city has a population of a million and about 400 000 people commute into Brussels to work. Of these over 150 000 travel by car.

Brussels has a good public transport system. There are 19 tramway lines and 34 bus routes serving the city and its suburbs. A new underground line, the metro, was built in 1976 to serve the western suburbs, the central area, the EEC and the eastern section of the city (see Fig. 39.4). This line goes under the old city and has eased congestion, making it possible to convert some of the streets into pedestrian precincts. Special schemes to encourage people to use the metro have been introduced at some suburban metro stations. Large car parks have been built at these stations and low parking charges encourage people to **park and ride**.

To reduce the amount of through traffic, a ring road has been built linking all the motorways which converge on Brussels (see Fig. 39.4).

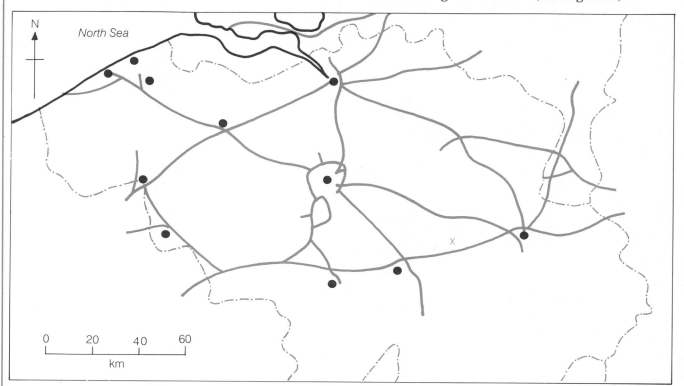

Fig. 39.3 The motorway network in Belgium

Activities

A Fig. 39.3 shows the Belgian motorway network.

(a) Make a copy of the map and, with the help of an atlas, add:
 (i) the names of the countries which border Belgium;
 (ii) the names of the towns shown by a dot.

(b) Which part of Belgium is not covered by the motorway network?

(c) How far is it from the capital to the Belgian coast along the motorway?

(d) What is the name of the river which is followed by the motorway marked X?

B Look at Fig. 39.4.

(a) Why has the ring motorway been built so far from the city centre?

(b) Imagine you own a restaurant visited mainly by tourists near the middle of the city centre. Which of the following proposals for alterations to the area would you like, and which would you dislike? Give your reasons in each case.
 (i) making a pedestrian precinct of the street in front of your restaurant
 (ii) building a fly-over from the city centre to provide a motorway link to the EEC building
 (iii) the banning of all private cars in the 'pentagon' zone of the city
 (iv) pulling down old buildings near the Grand Place (central square) to make way for a multi-storey car park.

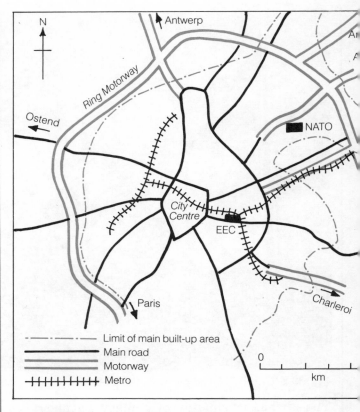

Fig. 39.4 Roads in and around Brussels

C The chart (Fig. 39.5) shows the means of transport used by commuters and school pupils in Brussels.

(a) What are the main differences between the means of transport used by the two groups of people?

(b) Suggest reasons for these differences.

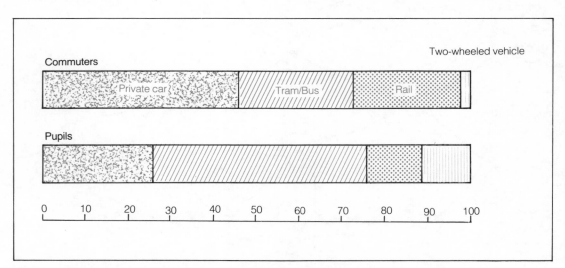

Fig. 39.5 Means of transport from home to work/school and return

Unit 40

Transport – suitability and costs

40.1 Different transport costs

A manufacturer or farmer who wants to sell his goods in cities in different parts of Europe must consider carefully how they should be transported. He will want to keep his transport costs as low as possible and also make sure that his products arrive at the right time and in good condition.

For smaller quantities of high value goods such as expensive jewellery or orchids, air freight is best because it is fast and the amount of time during which there is a risk of the goods being stolen or spoiled is short. Air freight is too expensive for very many goods and farm products, and other means of transport must be used.

Water transport is slow and best suited to bulky goods which are heavy and have relatively low value for each tonne transported. Consequently iron ore, chemicals, sand and gravel, oil and cereals make up the bulk of cargoes on the waterways.

For manufacturers selling clothes, cars, refrigerators and many of the other goods and foodstuffs we use every day there is a choice between using road or rail transport to reach their customers.

40.2 Choosing between road and rail

The French firm of Mobalpa makes kitchen units (cupboards, worktops, shelving etc), in a factory at Thônes, a small settlement in the French Alps about 20 kilometres from the town of Annecy. Annecy has railway links and is on the French motorway network. The firm's products are sold mainly in France, West Germany, Britain, Switzerland and the Benelux countries (Belgium, the Netherlands and Luxembourg).

The kitchen units are fairly light, but are bulky and must be packed in cardboard cartons before leaving the factory. These cartons are stacked into large metal containers which are loaded on to trucks. The firm uses road transport instead of rail because it is more convenient. It has a fleet of 50 heavy-duty trucks.

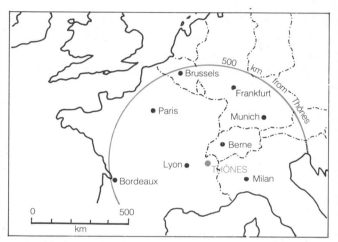

Fig. 40.2 The location of the Mobalpa factory

Fig. 40.1 A container lorry at Smithfield Market, London

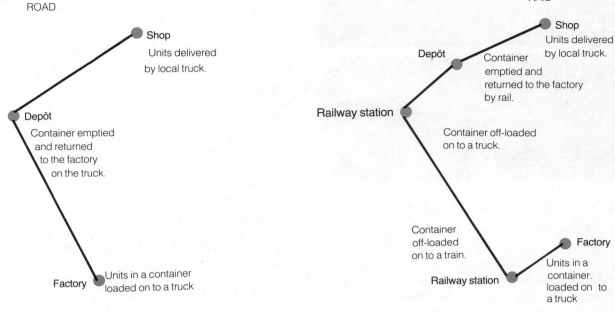

Fig. 40.3 Moving goods by road and rail

As Fig. 40.3 shows, one advantage of using road transport is that there are fewer transfers from one type of transport to another. On the other hand, road transport over long distances is more expensive than the railways. However, Mobalpa knows that many of its customers live within a 500 km radius of the factory.

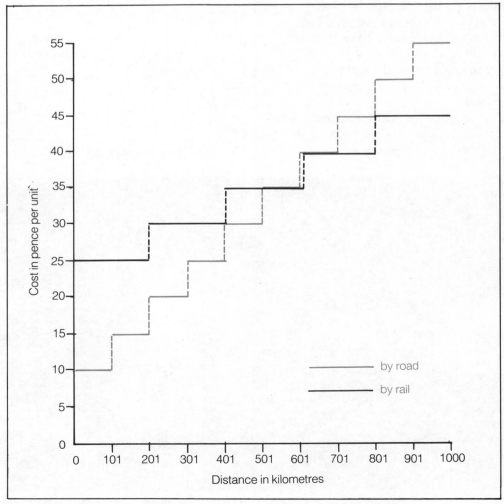

Fig. 40.4 Transport costs from Munich to other European towns and cities

Activities

A You are the director of a freight forwarding firm in Basel, Switzerland, and you are asked to arrange suitable transport for the freight which is listed below. For each item decide which is the most suitable form of transport and list the reasons for your decisions. Basel is shown on Fig. 37.1; it has an airport, is at the head of navigation of the River Rhine, and is on the European motorway and rail networks.

(a) Four rare monkeys which are to be sent to Amsterdam Zoo

(b) 1000 tonnes of building stone for new office blocks in Stuttgart

(c) 200 cuckoo clocks for a shop in Paris

(d) 100 tonnes of machinery for a new power station near Turin

(e) 40 cartons of Gruyère cheese for a wholesaler in Lyon

Draw a map to show the routes you have chosen for these items of freight.

B Fig. 40.4 shows the differences in cost between carrying freight by road and by rail from Munich to other cities in Europe. Although in theory costs change with every kilometre the goods are carried, the actual costs charged are calculated more simply, as the graph shows. By road the cost charged is for each 100 kilometres or part of 100 kilometres travelled, so a journey of 100 kilometres costs 10p per unit, the same as a journey of only 5 kilometres. By rail the cost charged is for each 200 kilometres, or part of 200 kilometres travelled. A journey of 250 kilometres is therefore charged at the rate of 30p per unit (the 400 kilometre rate). A brewer in Munich wants to send 100 units of beer to each of the cities listed in Table 40.1

City	Distance from Munich (km)
Amsterdam	828
Basel	394
Belgrade	993
Berlin	604
Cologne	579
Frankfurt	408
Hamburg	876
Hanover	674
Milan	466
Zurich	308

Table 40.1

(a) Draw a map and mark on Munich and these 10 cities.

(i) Draw straight lines from Munich to each city.

(ii) Mark in blue those cities to which it is cheaper to send beer by rail, and in red those where road transport is more economical. Use both colours if the costs are identical.

(b) What would be the cost of sending 1000 units of beer to Frankfurt by (i) road; (ii) rail?

(c) How much more expensive would it be to send 500 units of beer to Hamburg by road instead of by rail?

Industry

Unit 41

Mining

41.1 Iron ore

Europe is well endowed with iron ore; there are small deposits in many countries and larger amounts in the USSR, Sweden, Spain and France. Iron ore varies in quality according to the amount of iron it contains. An ore with more than 50 per cent iron content is a **high-grade ore**, whereas one containing between 30 per cent and 50 per cent is called a **lean ore**, or low-grade.

Outside the USSR the largest deposits in Europe are in northern Sweden where the ore is high-grade, containing between 60 per cent and 70 per cent iron.

Iron ore also contains other minerals such as silica, lime and phosphorus. These are known as impurities and have to be removed. At one time ore containing phosphorus could not be used because it made the iron very brittle. Then in 1878 the Basic process was invented by Bessemer and phosphoric ores could be used in blast furnaces. The iron ore deposits in northern Sweden contain phosphorus whereas those in Spain and France do not.

Iron ore is heavy and bulky and transport costs can be very high. Water transport is cheapest over long distances but European iron ore deposits are not on the coast or close to navigable rivers, so rail transport must be used for part of the journey. In recent years transport costs have been reduced by treating the ore before it leaves the mines. This process, called enrichment, removes some of the waste rock, increasing the iron content of the ore. The ore is also concentrated into pellets which makes it easier to transport.

41.2 Mining iron ore in Sweden

Sweden produces 22 million tonnes of iron ore each year. By far the largest output, 90 per cent, comes from within the Arctic Circle at Kiruna and Gällivare. The remainder comes from mines in the Bergslagen region of central Sweden near Grängesberg and Dannemora.

The Bergslagen ores have been worked for hundreds of years and a local iron industry grew up using charcoal to heat the metal. Today steel is made using hydro-electric power and works specializing in quality steels have grown up in the area. Ore is also sent by rail to Oxelösund south of Stockholm for use in the large steel works in the town.

The huge ore deposits in the north of Sweden are in Lappland, a region remote from the rest of the country. Because the ores are phosphoric they were not used until the end of the nineteenth century. The largest ore field is at Kiruna, a town which has grown up to provide housing and other services for the mining community. Smaller fields are located at Gällivare and Svappavaara.

A single track railway runs from the Swedish coast at Luleå to the Norwegian port of Narvik. It is used for carrying ore from the mines to these ports. Most of the Kiruna ore goes to Narvik while that from Gällivare is sent mainly to Luleå. Unlike the Bergslagen region, there are no steel works near the ore fields. The only steel works is on the coast at Luleå using ore from Gällivare and hydro-electricity from a number of inland power stations.

Fig. 41.1 Kiruna town and mine, Sweden

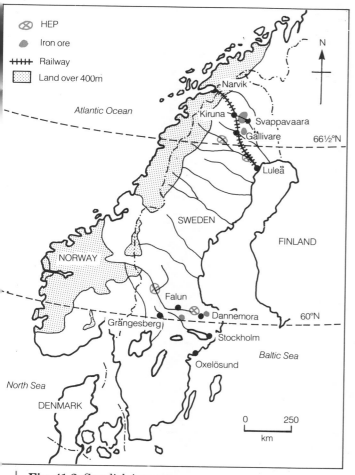

Fig. 41.2 Swedish iron ore

Some iron ore is shipped from Luleä to steel works in central Sweden but most is exported via Narvik to other countries of Western Europe, especially West Germany, Belgium/Luxembourg, France and the UK.

Activities

A Look at the following information in Tables 41.1 and 41.2 about the two iron mining regions

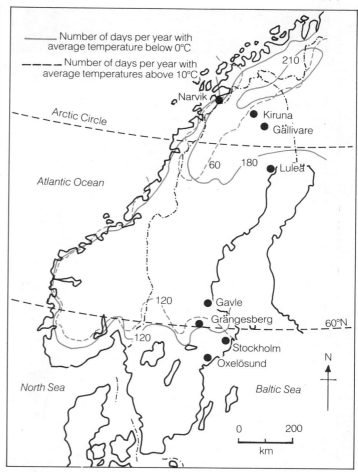

Fig. 41.3 Winter/summer temperatures in Scandinavia

in Sweden. With the help of the information and Figs. 41.2, 41.3, and 41.4 answer the questions which follow.

(a) For how many months are the average temperatures in Kiruna below freezing?

(b) Approximately how many more days are there with temperatures below freezing at Kiruna compared with Grängesberg?

(c) For how many months do plants grow at Grängesberg?

(d) How many months is Luleä harbour closed by ice?

°C	J	F	M	A	My	J	Jy	A	S	O	N	D
Grängesberg	−3	−3	−2	3	8	14	17	16	12	6	2	−2
Kiruna	−11	−12	−8	−2	5	10	14	11	6	−2	−9	−10

Table 41.1 Temperature figures for Grängesberg and Kiruna

Harbour	Closed		Reason
	From	To	
Gävle	mid-Feb	mid-March	⎫ Baltic is not very salty so freezes easily
Luleä	mid-Dec	mid-May	⎭
Narvik	—	—	Warm water of North Atlantic Drift flows along coast
Oxelösund	—	—	Too far south for ice to be a problem

Table 41.2 The times of year when harbours are closed by ice

Activities continued

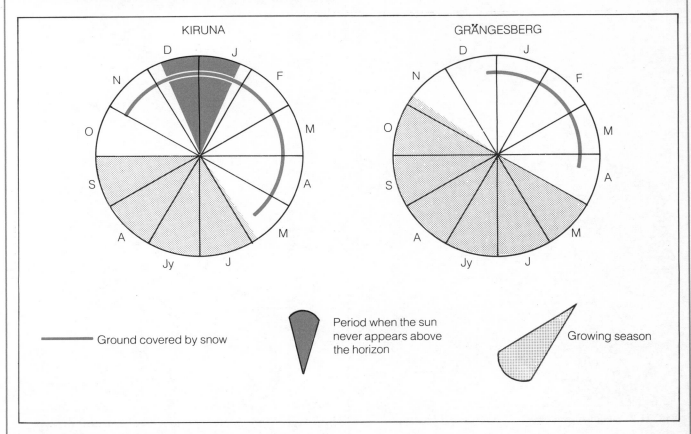

Fig. 41.4 Differences during a year between Kiruna and Grängesberg

(e) What is the latitude of Grängesberg?
(f) Approximately how far is Kiruna from Stockholm in a straight line?

B (a) Name the Swedish settlements which are inside the Arctic Circle.
(b) Why must the street lights be kept on all day for part of the year at Kiruna?

C Which one of the following is the correct explanation for exporting most of the iron ore from Swedish Lappland via the port of Narvik instead of via Luleå?

(a) The railway journey from Kiruna is shorter to Narvik than to Luleå and the line follows fairly level ground.
(b) Most of the journey is downhill, so little energy is used up by the trains.
(c) The port of Narvik is open all through the year.
(d) There is no outlet from the Baltic to the North Sea.
(e) The trains can earn money on the return journey by carrying Norwegian tourists.

D Both Kiruna and Grängesberg are modern towns with good housing and other facilities. Imagine you are a skilled mining engineer and have been offered a job at Grängesberg at 200 000 Swedish kroner per year, and a similar job at Kiruna at 270 000 kroner per year. Discuss the advantages and disadvantages of living in each of these towns and give reasons for the one you select to work in.

E List reasons why iron and steel works have grown up close to the iron ore fields in central Sweden but not near the iron ore fields of Swedish Lappland.

Unit 42

Iron and steel

42.1 Changes in the cost of making steel

In Book 1, Unit 44, iron ore and coke were named as the main raw materials needed to make steel. In an iron and steel works these raw materials are first used to produce pig iron which is then converted into steel.

The cost of these raw materials, together with the cost of the processes and the wages of the workers (labour costs), help to determine the cost of the finished steel and the price at which it must be sold for the firm to make a profit.

During the last twenty years changes have taken place in the steel industry which are mainly the result of changes in the costs of the inputs.

Raw material sources

The lean iron ore of Lorraine in France has become more expensive than higher grade iron ore from Brazil, Canada, Liberia and Australia. Swedish ore from Kiruna is still used although less is being exported. Coal from the Ruhr and the Franco-Belgian coalfield has been partly replaced by cheaper coal from the United States. Like the iron ore, the coal is carried in bulk carriers at very low costs.

Labour costs

Many iron and steel works have been built in recent years in developing countries such as Brazil, North Korea, China and India. These works are frequently close to raw material sources and have cheaper labour costs than European works. As a result they are able to undersell European producers and make labour costs in Europe relatively high.

Processes

Many European works use out-of-date processes which increase costs. Technological changes have increased the importance of steel making which uses a blast of oxygen; older methods have become less efficient. More scrap metal can be used in modern furnaces which again reduces costs.

42.2 Changes in location and output

Forty years ago most iron and steel plants were located close to raw material sources. As Fig. 42.1 shows, the position has changed. Changes in costs, together with a fall in the demand for steel, have resulted in the closing of many plants inland, and a shift to coastal locations where cheaper raw materials can be unloaded directly into the works.

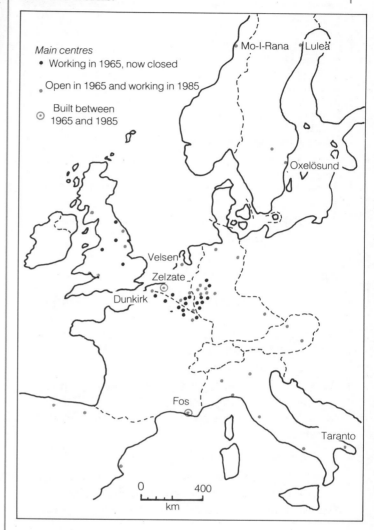

Fig. 42.1 Iron and steel centres in Western Europe, 1965 – 1985

Activities

A Look at Fig. 42.1.

(a) How many of the main iron and steel centres in 1985 are on the coast or within 50 kilometres of the coast?

(b) How many works, which were open in 1965 and have been closed since, were on the coast or within 50 kilometres of it?

(c) Which two iron and steel works have been built since 1965?

(d) What does the map tell us about changes in the location of iron and steel works since 1965?

Activities *continued*

B

Country	1974	1982	% change
Belgium/Luxembourg	22.6	12.3	−45.6
Denmark	0.5	0.8	
West Germany	53.4	35.9	
France	27.0	18.4	
Italy	23.8	24.7	
Netherlands	5.8	3.4	
UK	22.3	13.7	

Table 42.1 Steel output in EEC countries (million tonnes)

To find the percentage change in output between 1974 and 1982 use the formula:

$$\frac{\text{Difference between outputs in 1982 and 1974}}{\text{output in 1974}} \times \frac{100}{1}\%$$

e.g. for Belgium/Luxembourg 22.6 − 12.3

$$\text{Percentage change} = \frac{10.3}{22.6} \times \frac{100}{1} = -45.6\%$$

(a) Copy the table and complete it by working out the percentage changes for the other six EEC steel producing countries.

(b) Which country has reduced its steel output most drastically since 1974?

(c) Which countries have increased their output since 1974?

C   The Velsen iron and steel works

The Netherlands has one iron and steel works at Velsen at the seaward end of the North Sea Canal. The works (sometimes called the Ijmuiden works) started with blast furnaces to make pig iron in 1924. Steel furnaces were added in 1939 and in recent years it has been modernized with furnaces using the oxygen process. The harbour has been deepened to take bulk ore carriers of 50 000 tonnes and the works is one of the largest and most efficient in the EEC.

Country of origin	Iron ore (million tonnes)
Sweden	1.57
Brazil	1.38
Canada	1.17
Spain	.82
Liberia	.16
Others	1.06
Total	6.16

Table 42.2 Iron ore imports at Velsen

Look at Fig. 42.2 and the information given above.

(a) Where would iron ore and coal for the Velsen blast furnaces have been obtained from fifty years ago?

(b) What means of transport would have been used to move coal to the blast furnaces?

(c) What are the advantages of the location of the Velsen works at the present time for:
 (i) Obtaining overseas iron ore?
 (ii) Sending steel goods to Amsterdam?
 (iii) Sending steel plate to the shipyards at Schiedam and Rotterdam?

(d) What kind of transport might be used to supply the Philips works at Eindhoven with sheet steel which is needed in the manufacture of washing machines and other household appliances?

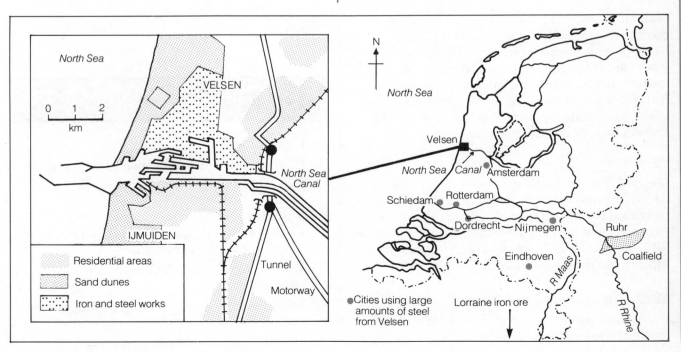

Fig. 42.2 The Velsen iron and steel works

Unit 43

Oil refining

43.1 Europe's oil supplies

Western Europe obtains about 90 per cent of its oil supplies from overseas, particularly from countries in the Middle East. The other 10 per cent comes from oil resources under the North Sea or from small oil fields on land such as that near Groningen in the north of the Netherlands and Parentis in south-west France.

Crude oil is a thick, treacle-like liquid which varies in its composition from one oil field to another. Oil from the Middle East is 'heavy' and needs more processing to obtain the lighter products such as petrol. By contrast, North Sea oil is 'lighter' and contains higher proportions of petrol and gas.

Oil refineries are places where the crude oil is treated to separate the heavier oils such as lubricating oil and diesel from the lighter paraffin and petrol. In an oil refinery the crude oil is heated by steam in a tall tower. The products have different boiling points and can be drawn off as 'fractions'. The lightest fractions are the gases which can be stored in cylinders and used as fuels. Petrol and paraffin are used by cars and aircraft while the heavier diesel and fuel oils are used in engines and for firing furnaces. Another product, naphtha, provides chemicals for the petro-chemical industry. All these products are further refined to remove impurities such as sulphur.

43.2 Oil refinery location

The most economical way of moving crude oil from the oil fields to the market is by large tankers, the largest of which can carry half a

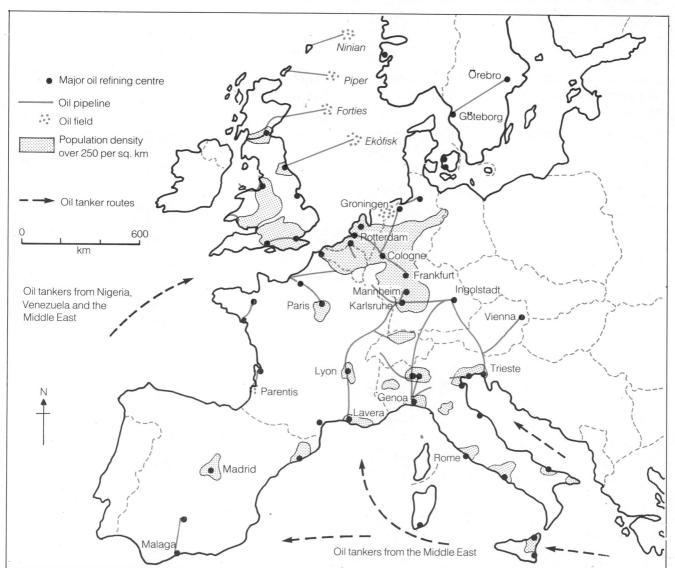

Fig. 43.1 European oil refinery centres and oil pipelines

million tonnes of oil. These huge tankers can only enter ports with deep water and much space is needed on land for tanks where the crude oil can be temporarily stored. Oil refineries have therefore grown up where there is deep water close inshore and there is plenty of cheap land available for storage tanks and the processing plant. Since markets for the crude oil products may be some way inland from the refinery, good communications to these markets are also necessary. Oil refineries do not need to be located near a fuel source such as coal since they can use waste gas for their heating needs.

Fig. 43.1 shows that most oil refineries are on the coast. The map also shows that some refineries have been built inland and are connected to coastal refineries by oil pipelines. The trend towards inland refineries contrasts with the coastal movement of steel works which was described in Unit 42. Inland refineries are a recent development, the result of:

1 improved methods of constructing steel pipelines to carry the crude oil;

2 the rapid increase in demand for oil products in the heavily populated regions of north-west Europe;

3 reductions in the cost of transporting crude oil compared with the cost of transporting oil products;

4 increased economic cooperation between the countries of Western Europe, particularly those in the EEC.

43.3 Oil refineries in the South of France

The Etang de Berre is a large shallow lagoon joined to the Mediterranean by a narrow channel. Land around the lagoon is low and marshy and ideal for large-scale industrial development.

This area is an extension of the port of Marseille which lacks suitable sites for industrial development nearer the city. A channel ten metres deep allows tankers to reach the Berre refinery on the lagoon. In 1962 a pipeline was opened between the Lavéra refinery and Strasbourg and Karlsruhe on the Rhine.

The largest and most important developments have been west of the lagoon near Fos where a fourth refinery has been built by Esso, as well as a large steel works and a number of other manufacturing plants.

Activities

A

Countries	% supplied
Persian Gulf countries	61.2
Libya	7.4
Nigeria	5.4
USSR	5.1
Egypt	2.9
Venezuela	2.8
Others	15.2

Table 43.1 Sources of crude oil imports to EEC countries

Look at Fig. 43.1 and the table above.

(a) Why is there a large number of oil refineries along the shores of the Mediterranean?
(b) Why is Karlsruhe in West Germany supplied with oil by pipeline from Lavéra in southern France rather than by a pipeline from Rotterdam which is much nearer?
(c) Why have nearly all the inland refineries been built in areas with high population densities?
(d) Suggest the route for one additional pipeline to supply an area of high population.
(e) In which city should a refinery be built to use oil carried by the pipeline?

B Use an atlas and Table 43.1 to answer these questions.

(a) Find the Etang de Berre. What is the name of the river which flows into the Mediterranean to the west of the Etang?
(b) Name three countries on the Persian Gulf.
(c) Which two routes can oil tankers use to carry oil from the Persian Gulf to Fos?
(d) Which Mediterranean countries will send crude oil to the refineries shown on the map?

Use Fig. 43.2 to help answer these questions.

(e) Why have chemical firms built factories close to the refineries?
(f) List the reasons why Esso chose the site near Fos for an oil refinery.

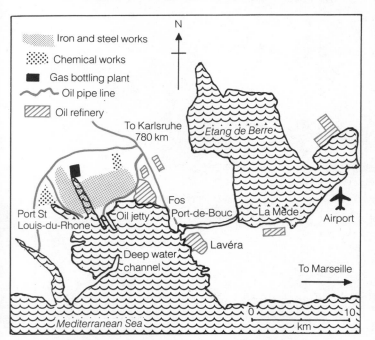

Fig. 43.2 Oil refineries and industries near the Etang de Berre

Unit 44

Industrial concentration

44.1 The heavy industrial triangle

The photograph overleaf shows part of the town of Douai on the coalfield of north-east France which belongs to the largest concentration of industry in Western Europe. This concentration includes the Ruhr coalfield of West Germany, the coalfield of north-east France and Belgium, and the iron ore region of Lorraine.

The industrial region grew up in the nineteenth century when industries depended upon coal for their power and on local raw materials such as iron ore. Canals and railways were built to link the factories to their raw material supplies and to waterways such as the Rhine and Meuse.

An iron and steel industry developed and other heavy industries such as engineering followed. People were attracted to the region and the population rapidly grew. The heavy industries attracted other industries such as engineering and chemicals which used iron and steel products or by-products. As towns and cities expanded new factories were built which needed to be near the market because their goods were perishable or expensive to send long distances. As a result food processing firms such as bakeries and other market-based factories grew up.

The increased population, with money to spend from regular wages, attracted a variety of service industries including banks, insurance firms and department stores.

As Fig. 44.1 shows, the industrial region forms a triangle which has acted as a magnet for industrial growth. While it became more profitable for industries to develop inside the triangle, in other regions lack of opportunities encouraged people to move away and the regions became relatively poor. The prosperous region is called the **core area** while the poorer regions are known as **the periphery**.

44.2 Core and periphery in Britain

The Industrial Revolution started in Britain and the pattern of development was similar to that which occurred later in north-west Europe. Heavy industries grew up on the coalfields of S Wales, the Midlands, the North-East, North-West and Central Scotland. People moved to these areas to work and they became core areas. By contrast people left the rural areas of Scotland, the Pennines and Central Wales and these became the periphery.

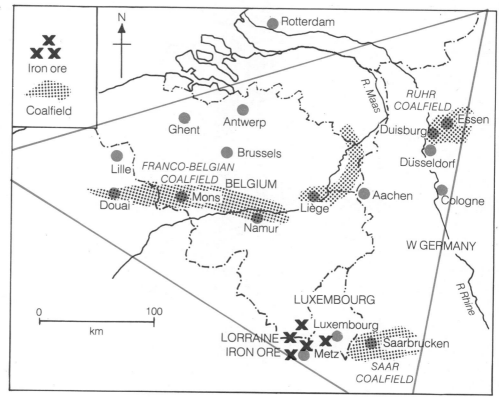

Fig. 44.1 The heavy industrial triangle

Fig. 44.2
Industrial town
of Douai

Fig. 44.3 Sketch map
of part of Douai

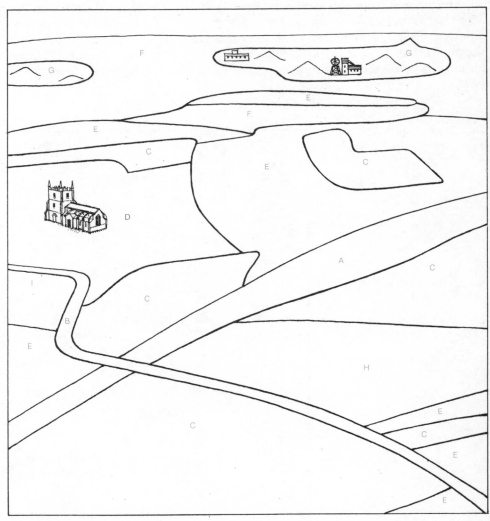

44.3 Present day problems in the industrial triangle

Today the heavy industrial triangle has lost some of its importance. Iron ore deposits on the coalfields have been worked out and cheaper ores can be imported from overseas. Less coal is needed as more use is made of oil and gas. Nevertheless, the Ruhr still produces good quality coking coal and other industries have moved into the triangle as the heavy industries have declined. The triangle is the most prosperous industrial region in Western Europe but the rapid unplanned development of the nineteenth century has resulted in urban congestion and industrial pollution on a large scale.

Firms are not keen to move out of the region. Having spent a great deal of money on buildings and other facilities, they have stayed in the triangle after their original reasons for choosing the site have disappeared. They stay because it is expensive to move and find a suitable labour force elsewhere. This is called **industrial inertia** and partly explains why nineteenth century industrial concentrations like the triangle remain important manufacturing regions today.

Activities

A Look at the photograph opposite and Fig. 44.3 which shows some of the features in the photograph. These features are identified by letters and are listed below, but not in the right order.

coal mines; railway tracks and sidings; open farmland; factories; housing; graveyard; town centre; woodland; main road.

(a) Make a copy of Fig. 44.3 without the letters.
(b) Shade or colour in the features in the list and annotate your sketch map.
(c) Has the area grown up haphazardly or been carefully planned? Give reasons for your answer.

B Fig. 44.4 is a diagram showing how industrial concentrations develop.

Make a copy of the diagram and fill in the rectangles with suitable headings to match the examples which have been given.

C Do you live in a core or peripheral area? Give reasons for your answer.

Fig. 44.4 Industrial concentration

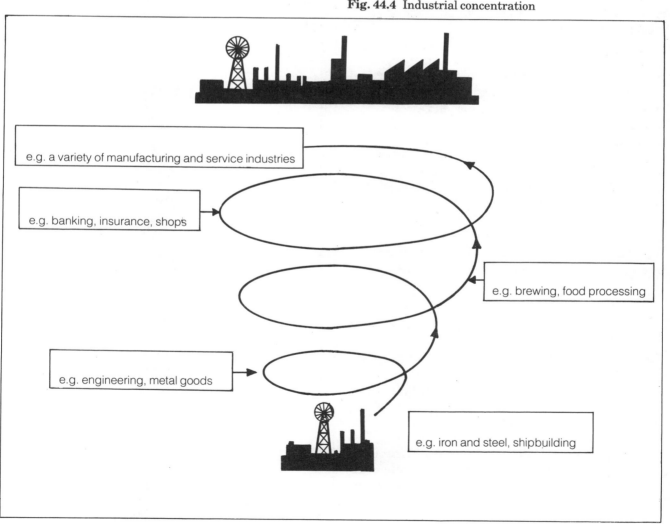

Unit 45

Industrial trends

45.1 New core areas

Much modern industry is concerned with producing relatively 'light' goods which use small amounts of raw materials and can be located at a variety of suitable sites, where electricity is available to provide power for the machinery.

The watch industry of Switzerland is an example of an industry which is not close to its markets or its raw materials. Modern watches often contain electronic components and are delicate instruments requiring a highly skilled labour force. Some firms make the small component parts, others the tools which are needed, while others specialise in assembling the watches. The industry is confined to a small region in the Jura mountains and at Geneva where skilled labour is available.

Other Swiss industries such as textiles and engineering have grown up in the same part of the country and form a small core region with industrial concentration based on the production of high-quality goods using imported raw materials, skilled labour and electricity from hydro-electric power stations in the Alps.

Although improvements in communications and the widespread availability of electricity, oil and gas have resulted in a much greater dispersal of industry, new industrial concentrations are also appearing. Like Switzerland, many European countries have developed small core regions where high population densities attract new industries at the expense of peripheral regions.

45.2 Dispersed industries

The pull of the coalfields is no longer strong enough to attract modern industries. Many industries can be sited at a variety of locations provided there is easy access to the raw materials, power and labour that are required. The European aircraft industry is an example of industrial dispersal with hundreds of different component parts being made in other locations in Europe and overseas. One of the largest assembly points for these components is at Toulouse where the European Airbus is produced.

Fig. 45.1 Assembly worker in watch factory, Switzerland

As Fig. 45.3 shows, firms in other regions must rely on good communications to move their products to Toulouse. The wings, for example, are air-freighted from Bremen to the factory in south-west France by way of St Nazaire.

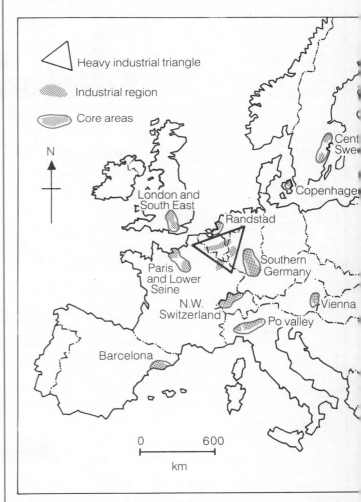

Fig. 45.2 Core areas in Western Europe

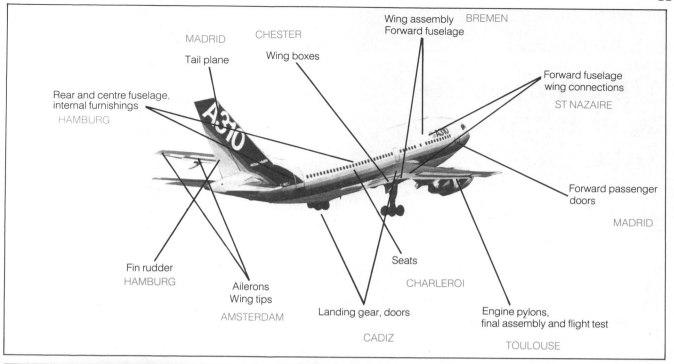

Fig. 45.3 Where major parts of the A310 Airbus are made

Activities

A Give reasons why the following benefit from setting up businesses in core areas.

(a) fashion designers   (b) watch makers
(c) printers   (d) bottle makers

B One of the problems of industrial concentration in core areas is pollution. This cutting (Fig. 45.4) from *The Times* dated 19th January 1985 describes a smog alert.

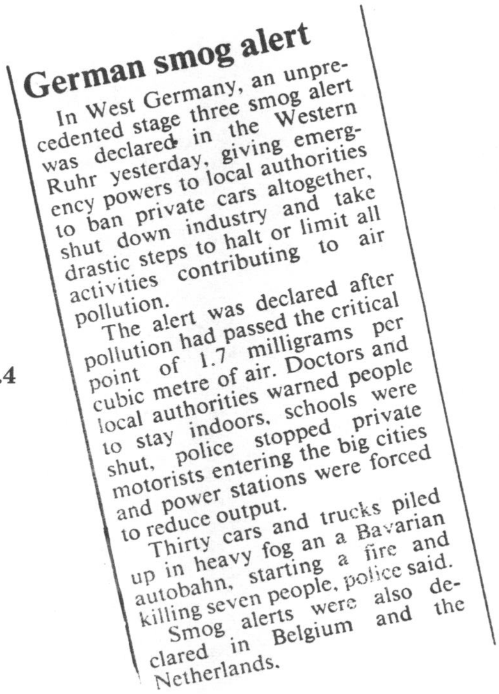

Fig. 45.4

German smog alert

In West Germany, an unprecedented stage three smog alert was declared in the Western Ruhr yesterday, giving emergency powers to local authorities to ban private cars altogether, shut down industry and take drastic steps to halt or limit all activities contributing to air pollution.

The alert was declared after pollution had passed the critical point of 1.7 milligrams per cubic metre of air. Doctors and local authorities warned people to stay indoors, schools were shut, police stopped private motorists entering the big cities and power stations were forced to reduce output.

Thirty cars and trucks piled up in heavy fog an a Bavarian autobahn, starting a fire and killing seven people, police said.

Smog alerts were also declared in Belgium and the Netherlands.

(a) Why were motorists prevented from entering the big cities?
(b) Why were power stations forced to reduce output?
(c) Why were people warned to stay indoors?
(d) What other forms of pollution can be caused by industry?

C How could the various things that cause pollution in the western Ruhr be controlled so that the need for smog alerts becomes less?

D Look at Fig. 45.3.
The wing components made at Chester are sent to Bremen where parts of the wing are assembled. They are then sent to St Nazaire in France for further additions before being flown to Toulouse.

(a) Draw a map of Western Europe to show the centres supplying parts for the Airbus.
(b) Show as a simple network diagram the routes taken by these components to reach Toulouse.
(c) Name one other industry which uses many components and assembles the product in large factories using an assembly line.

Unit 46

Governments and industrial location

46.1 Helping the peripheral regions

The governments of countries in Western Europe are anxious to even out the distribution of wealth so that regions which are not prosperous will get a fairer share of the nation's wealth. In Unit 33 we saw the contrast between the core area of northern Italy and the poorer peripheral area of the Mezzogiorno. Some of the ways the Italian government is spending money to improve the South were described, including the development of new industrial centres.

The wealth of core areas comes mainly from their manufacturing and service industries and governments are therefore anxious to attract new industries and services to the periphery. The only work available is usually on the land where output is low and inefficient. People leave these regions to find work elsewhere, usually in core areas which become more congested and over-populated.

Although problems at the periphery differ from area to area, most governments have used broadly similar ways to attract manufacturing and service industries. The main methods are:

1 giving grants to firms which set up factories in peripheral areas

2 not taxing new firms for a period of time while they become established

3 building factories which can be rented cheaply by industrialists

4 giving loans to firms at low rates of interest

5 moving government departments into poorer regions

These methods provide incentives which encourage firms to choose peripheral areas for their businesses. Manufacturing and service industries are discouraged from going to areas of high employment by various constraints. These include:

1 refusing permission for firms to build new factories or offices

2 taxing firms more heavily in cities and core areas

46.2 Aid from the European Economic Community

The countries of the EEC contribute money towards funds which are used to help poor regions within the Community. The most important source of help is the Regional Development Fund. Money from this fund helped to build the Autostrada del Sole (Unit 33). Another source of money is the European Investment Bank which grants loans for projects in less-developed regions.

Fig. 46.1 Citroën car factory, Rennes

Fig. 46.2 Brittany – industries and services developed

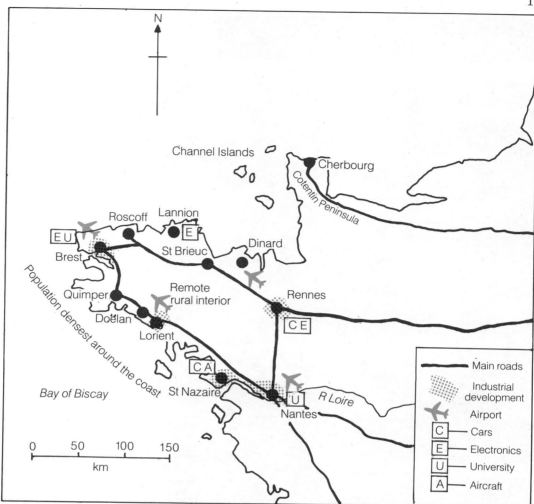

46.3 A French peripheral region – Brittany

As Fig. 45.2 shows, the major core region in France is Paris and the lower Seine valley.

For centuries Paris has dominated France as the most important centre in the country for commerce, industry, administration and education. This has caused a gap between the wealth and power of the capital and the rest of the country.

The poorly developed areas of France are to the west of a line from Paris to Marseille and include Brittany, the most remote of the regions.

Fig. 46.2 shows some of the industries and services which have been developed in Brittany, to provide alternative employment to work on the land and to halt the constant drift of people moving out of the region for jobs.

With government help Citroën has built a large car plant at Rennes and the state has also encouraged electronics industries in the region. Jobs in education and administration have been made at Brest and Nantes by setting up large regional universities. Nantes and St Nazaire have been made into metropolitan regions with expansion of industrial, commercial and cultural interests to help offset the attraction of Paris.

Activities

A Fig. 46.3 shows the village of Doëlan about 10 kilometres west of Lorient on the south coast of Brittany. Like many small ports along this coast, the main forms of employment are fishing (some fishing boats can be seen in the harbour), catering for small numbers of tourists and working on farms inland.

Imagine you are the owner of a small electronics firm making components for telephones which are assembled in Paris. Your works in Paris is in a very cramped building and employs 30 people. You wish to expand the business and employ twice as many, but you have been refused permission to extend your factory in Paris. Instead you have been offered a building in Doëlan. The building can be seen on the right of the photo in the foreground overlooking the harbour. It has a large chimney behind it.

To encourage you to move to this site and expand, the government will pay 60% of your removal costs and give you a grant to help set up the business in Doëlan, train new staff and so on.

The alternative possibility is to take a site

Activities continued

Fig. 46.3 Doëlan, Southern Brittany

about 100 kilometres to the east of Paris at Sézanne. At this site, just outside the core area, no government help will be given.

After studying the costs carefully you find they can be summarized as follows:

Cost in francs	Doëlan	Sézanne
Cost of moving machinery, workers etc	50 000 less 60%	40 000

Cost per month (francs)	Doëlan	Sézanne
Materials	10 000	10 000
Transport	25 000	15 000
Labour	400 000	430 000
Power	5 000	5 000
Rent of site	5 000	5 000
	(0.5 hectare)	(0.1 hectare)
Government grant for 12 months, amount per month	10 000	—

Table 46.1

(a) Why would transport costs be higher at Doëlan?

(b) Why would labour costs be lower at Doëlan than at Sézanne?

(c) Why would the removal costs be lower at Doëlan than at Sézanne?

(d) At the end of the first month, where would the total production costs be lower?

(e) How much would be saved in production costs at the end of the first year by choosing the cheaper site?

(f) Where would costs be lowest during the second year? By how much?

B (a) Imagine you are a worker at the Paris factory. List the advantages and disadvantages of going to live in Doëlan.

(b) Discuss how the following people living in Doëlan might react when they hear that the large building overlooking the harbour is to become an electronics factory, employing some local people as well as workers brought from Paris:
  (i) the village lawyer
 (ii) a local fisherman
(iii) a housewife with two teenage children
(iv) a shopkeeper who depends on the summer tourist trade for his living

Unit 47

The tourist industry

47.1 The importance of tourism

The tourist trade is a service industry which provides work in hotels and restaurants, transport services, shops, specialist tourist facilities and other services which are needed by tourists.

Tourism also boosts primary and manufacturing industries. Farmers and fishermen sell their produce to hotels and restaurants while building workers are needed to construct new hotels and tourist centres. People working in traditional craft industries such as weaving and wood carving can sell their goods as souvenirs to the visitors.

The main tourist regions of Europe are some way from the core industrial triangle. They form part of the periphery and in many cases are less developed and remote rural regions. People from the core area are attracted to the mountains, lakes and beaches for their holidays and to regions with warm, sunny weather. As a result the regions which are most popular with tourists are often in countries with low living standards in southern Europe. For these countries, such as Greece, Italy, Portugal and Spain, tourism is an essential part of the economy, providing much needed employment and a higher standard of living.

Other countries which already have a high standard of living such as Switzerland, Austria and Denmark also attract tourists and benefit from the money they spend.

The table below shows the number of tourist visitors from other countries in Europe and the population of the country visited.

Country	Tourists	Population of host country
Austria	8.2	7.6
Belgium	3.3	9.9
Denmark	3.4	5.1
France	26.0	54.2
West Germany	6.2	61.7
Greece	3.4	9.8
Italy	40.8	57.4
Portugal	6.8	9.9
Spain	37.5	37.9
Switzerland	4.7	6.3
UK	0.6	56.1

Table 47.1 Estimated number of tourists from other countries in Europe (millions), 1982

47.2 Davos – a Swiss resort

Fig. 47.1 is a summer view, looking over Klosters near the Swiss resort of Davos in the south-east of Switzerland. Davos is 1550 metres above sea level and the peaks in the area reach heights of over 3000 metres. Davos is one of the fifteen major tourist centres in Switzerland and it has been an important resort for over 100 years.

Tourism began in Switzerland in the last century with visits by wealthy people to climb and walk in the Alps. Since 1945 tourism has changed dramatically. Holidays with pay, cheaper transport, particularly by air, and package holidays have made it possible for the majority of working class people in other Western European countries to enjoy a holiday in towns like Davos.

Its location makes Davos both a winter and summer resort. The clear atmosphere and mountain air have also attracted fourteen clinics and sanatoria as well as a tuberculosis research centre to which patients are sent from all over the world. There are just over 100 hotels and guest houses which are used by about 160 000 visitors each year. This part of Switzerland is very popular with the Swiss themselves and nearly half the visitors are from other parts of Switzerland.

Switzerland's reputation for high tourist standards has been built up over a long period of time. In recent years the popularity of beach holidays in the Mediterranean has checked the expansion of the Swiss tourist industry and the government has stepped in to provide money for rural improvement schemes and to advertise the country's attractions.

Fig. 47.1 Klosters, near Davos

Activities

Fig. 47.2 Temperatures and precipitation in Davos

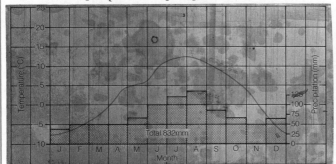

A Use the reference section of your local library to find a guide book on Switzerland which gives information about Davos. Use this information, together with the information in this Unit, to answer the following questions.

(a) What kind of activities does Davos offer to visitors who go there in summer?

(b) What activities are there for tourists in winter in Davos itself?

(c) How would the slopes of the mountains above the tree line be used in winter?

(d) How would visitors reach these slopes?

(e) Which months are likely to provide good winter sports conditions?

(f) What kind of weather would you expect if you visited Davos in August?

B Making a flow line map.

Flow line maps show movement from one place to another with the amount of movement being shown by the thickness of a line (see Fig. 34.2). Look at Fig. 47.3 and Table 47.2.

Home country	% of total
Austria	3
Belgium	5
France	13
West Germany	42
Netherlands	6
Italy	9
Spain	3
UK	12

Table 47.2 Visitors to Switzerland from other parts of Europe, 1982

To show these figures as flow lines:

(a) Make a copy of Fig. 47.3 but do not add the names of the countries as they may get in the way at this stage.

(b) Thicken each of the lines using the scale 1 mm = 3%.

(c) Add the names of the countries and percentage figures to your map, putting the percentage figures close to the flow lines.

(d) Make a copy of the key.

What problems are there in constructing the flow line?

Fig. 47.3 The homes of European visitors to Switzerland

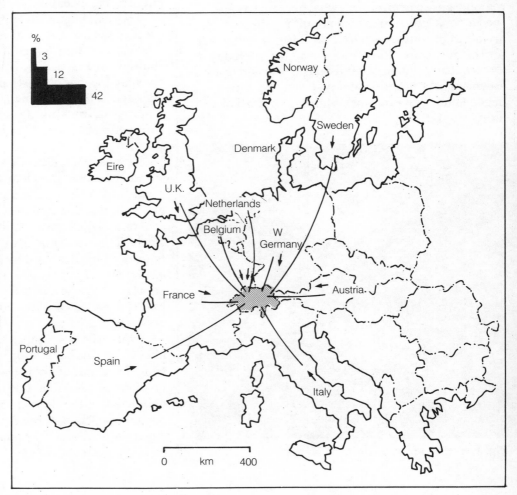

Unit 48

Problems of tourism

48.1 Sunshine and pollution

Tourism is an important contributor to the wealth of the countries of Europe which border the Mediterranean Sea, and it is playing an increasingly important part in the regional development of these areas as the number of tourists grow year by year. Although it is a valuable source of income, tourism is also a serious threat to the environment and the way of life of the people.

A particular problem in the Mediterranean is that it is almost a land-locked and tideless sea. Beaches which become polluted with rubbish and tar are not scoured by the next high tide and there are no ocean currents to carry away the waste. Over one hundred million tourists visit the Mediterranean coasts of Europe each year, doubling the number of local residents. About 85 per cent of the sewage from the coastal cities is poured into the sea without being fully treated. Waste is also discharged into the Mediterranean from large rivers like the Nile, Rhône, Po and Ebro, as well as from factories and oil refineries. Some 60 per cent to 70 per cent of the beaches are not 'safe' and swimming in many areas can be a health hazard.

The United Nations Environment Programme has been campaigning for less pollution but the full treatment of sewage is very expensive and some of the countries are relatively poor.

On land the impact of tourism can be very dramatic. Small, sleepy fishing ports can swiftly change into crowded resort towns backed by tall hotels and apartments.

Fig. 48.1

Fig. 48.2

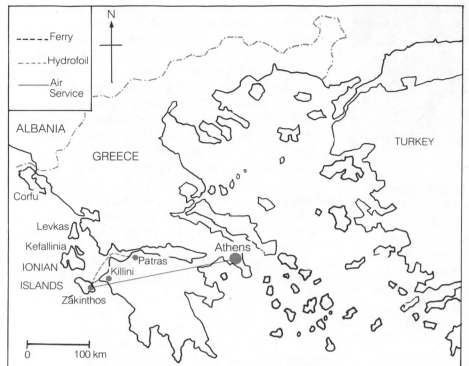

Fig. 48.3 The position of Zákinthos

48.2 The Island of Zákinthos

The Greek islands are very popular with holidaymakers and most of them are relatively undeveloped, but changes are beginning to take place.

As Fig. 48.3 shows, Zákinthos is one of the Ionian Islands about 250 kilometres west of Athens. The majority of the population works on the land growing vines, olives, fruit and wheat. Agricultural methods are backward and until the growth of tourism there was no other form of work available. As a result many people left the island, especially young people.

Tourism has not brought the extensive development which has occurred along the Spanish coast, but local people complain about many of the changes which have taken place. These changes can be grouped into costs and benefits. Costs to the island are the bad effects of tourism. For example, if the beaches on the south coast become crowded with tourists the marine turtles will no longer use them to lay their eggs in the sand. Benefits to the island are the good effects of tourism. One benefit has been that fewer people are leaving the island to find jobs elsewhere.

Activities

A

Benefits

1 Employment
2 Higher standard of living
3 Better roads
4 More places of entertainment
5 New ideas and interests
6 Restoration of old buildings, customs and traditions

Costs

1 Haphazard building
2 Rubbish
3 Polluted beaches
4 Land used for airfield etc is no longer available for farming
5 Increase in the number of vehicles
6 Crowded streets and beaches
7 Noisy night clubs and discos
8 Spread of souvenir shops
9 Altering customs and traditions to suit the tourists

(a) Write down the 9 costs in the list above and against each one describe what this cost means to the people who live on or visit the island.

For example: 1 Haphazard building – This spoils the landscape and takes away the natural beauty of the island.

(b) What steps should be taken by the local government of Zákinthos to check the increase in some of the 'costs' in the list?

(c) Discuss whether too much tourist development can, in time, destroy the tourist industry on Zákinthos.

B (a) Draw a graph to show the change in population of Zákinthos between 1951 and 1981 using the figures in Table 48.1.

Year	Population
1951	38 002
1961	35 509
1971	30 157
1981	30 014

Table 48.1 Zákinthos – population, 1951–1981

(b) What has happened to the total population?
(c) Has the change been a steady one, or is the rate of change altering?
(d) Explain any alteration you may have found.

C (a) Use the information in the climatic statistics given in Table 48.2 to decide the best months of the year to take a holiday on Zákinthos. Give reasons for your decision.

(b) What problems are there for the islanders if tourists only visit the island for a part of the year?

D Hold a discussion with your friends with each person taking one of the following rôles. The discussion, about tourism on the island, is between people living on Zákinthos who have seen the island change in recent years. An airport has been built, there is a hydrofoil service to the mainland and each year more tourists arrive by charter flights or independently to spend a week or more on the island. Some of the people are in favour of tourism, some are doubtful, while some are against having tourists on the island.

(a) a local builder
(b) a policeman
(c) a housewife who is concerned about the environment
(d) a girl who works in a bar
(e) a beach attendant
(f) a teenager still at school
(g) a fruit farmer
(h) a retired birdwatcher

After listening to the points of view of these people the class should vote on the motion, 'The people of Zákinthos are in favour of the development of tourism on the island'.

	J	F	M	A	My	J	Jy	A	S	O	N	D
Temperature (°C)	11.5	11.6	13.1	15.4	18.9	24.0	26.8	27.0	24.1	19.8	16.0	13.1
Rainfall (mm)	180	133	86	53	30	8	3	10	16	36	206	234
Average number of days with rain	13.8	12.5	10.5	8.0	6.0	3.6	0.8	1.4	4.4	9.9	13.1	16.5

Table 48.2 Climate statistics for Zákinthos

Fig. 48.4 The island of Zákinthos

Answers

Unit 1

A Albania – Tirana; Austria – Vienna; Belgium – Brussels; Bulgaria – Sofia; Czechoslovakia – Prague; Denmark – Copenhagen; E Germany – Berlin; Eire – Dublin; Finland – Helsinki; France – Paris; Greece – Athens; Hungary – Budapest; Italy – Rome; Luxembourg – Luxembourg; Netherlands – Amsterdam; Norway – Oslo; Poland – Warsaw; Portugal – Lisbon; Romania – Bucharest; Spain – Madrid; Sweden – Stockholm; Switzerland – Berne; UK – London; USSR – Moscow; W Germany – Bonn; Yugoslavia – Belgrade.

C **(b)** 23; **(c)** Eire, Norway, Denmark, E Germany, Czechoslovakia, W Germany, Luxembourg, Switzerland; **(d)** 2½ hrs.

D **(b)** Gibraltar; **(c)** 67%.

Unit 2

A **(a)** east-west; **(b)** Central Massif; **(c)** north; **(d)** 38 km; **(e)** Nantes.

B 1 (a) single track railway; **(b)** bushes, scrub; **(c)** track; **(d)** contour line; **(e)** cemetery; **(f)** spot height; **(g)** vines; **(h)** chimney; **(i)** factory.

2 (a) 303251; **(b)** 303254; **(c)** 309251; **(d)** 306254; **(e)** 301256; **(f)** 209255; **(g)** 409358; **(h)** 208158.

C **(a)** 116 m; **(b)** 114 m; **(c)** 116 m; **(d)** 114 m; **(e)** 118 m.

D **(a)** 1 km; **(b)** 1.5 km; **(c)** 1.2 km.

E **(a)** woods; **(b)** Sully-sur-Loire; **(c)** race tracks or sports arenas.

Unit 3

A **(a)** 460 m; **(b)** 110 m; **(c)** 570 m; **(d)** V shape.

B 1 (a) At 300 m the sketch will show 2 islands.
(b) At 500 m only the top of the higher mountain will appear.

C 1 (a) See Fig. 49.1.

C 2 (a) The boat must keep in water over 2 m deep;
(b) X is located on the NE coast where the 2 m contour reaches the coast; **(c)** 14 km.

D Fig. 49.2

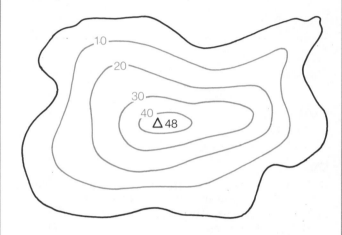

Fig. 49.2

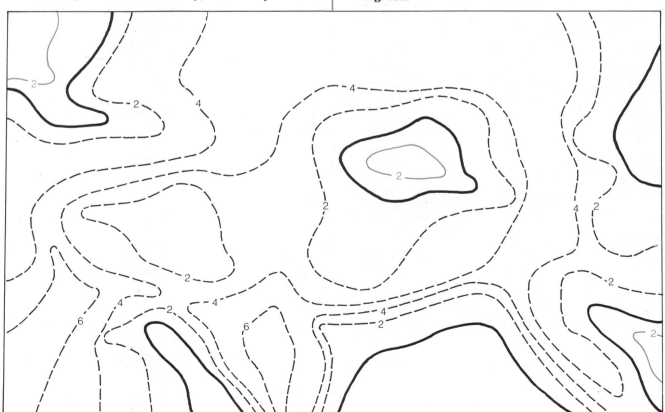

Fig. 49.1

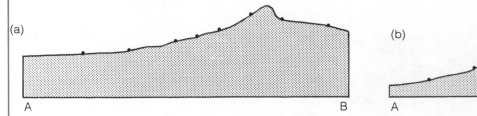

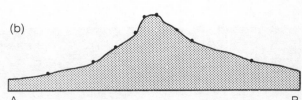

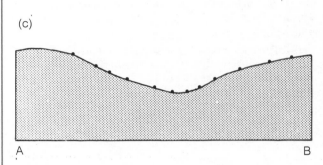

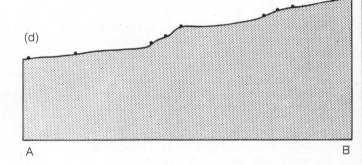

Fig. 49.3

Unit 4

See Fig. 49.3

E **(i)** E – F; **(ii)** A – B; **(iii)** C – D.

Unit 5

B **(a)** south-west; **(b)** as protection against the fine sand; **(c)** the fields have different shadings.

D **(a)** Cars are parked in a large car park; along both sides of some roads but not on the main beach road; on one road that crosses the dunes.
(b) People can be seen in large numbers on the beach and at the water's edge; there are also several in the swimming pool and walking along the roads; a few can be seen on the dunes.

Unit 6

A **(a)** 23½°S; **(b)** Tropic of Cancer; **(c)** **(i)** 60° N **(ii)** 23½° N **(iii)** 30° N **(iv)** 0° **(v)** 30° S; **(d)** **(i)** 30° E **(ii)** 0° **(iii)** 120° E **(iv)** 150° E **(v)** 15° W; **(e)** 7; **(f)** Prime Meridian.

B V – 23½° S, 135° E; W – 23½° N, 30° E; X – 0°, 15° E; Y – 45° N, 120° E; Z – 23½° N, 90° E.

C **(b)** *Gypsy*; **(c)** *Firefly*; **(d)** *Ranger*.

Unit 7

A **(a)** A; **(b)** The hot water stained with purple becomes lighter and rises. Near the surface where it is cooler it contracts, becomes heavier and sinks; **(c)** convection; **(d)** liquid rock in the mantle rises, spreads out, cools and sinks.

B **(a)** Eurasian and Indo-Australian plates
(b) Indo-Australian and Pacific plates
(c) Eurasian and African plates
(d) Nazca and American plates

Unit 8

A **(b)** Tristan da Cunha, Surtsey **(c)** Etna
(d) Krakatoa

C **(a)** Vesuvius **(b)** Krakatoa **(c)** Fuji-san
(d) Mont Pelée **(e)** Popocatepetl

D The answer should explain that Britain is not near plate margins whereas Japan is near the Eurasian and Pacific plate margins.

E Pressure from gas and magma built up in the vents. There was an explosion and one side of the volcano was blown away as ash and dust.

Unit 10

A **(f)** South-west
(g) Yes **(i)** they move from latitudes nearer the Equator towards the Pole
(ii) they are warmed by the North Atlantic Drift

B

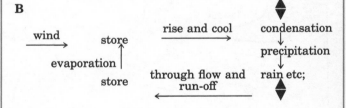

Unit 11

A **(a)** Westerlies
(b) Rain bearing westerlies bring summer rain
(c) Trade Winds are dry winds so there is no rain
(d) They bring dry conditions to the desert all through the year
(e) It has moist westerly winds all year

B **(a)** Against
(b) NE Trades; yes
(c) Fed up or depressed
(d) Sailors were becalmed and the ship could not proceed
(e) North-westerlies
(f) Cold Polar winds (which may also drive icebergs northwards)

Unit 12

A (a) Labrador; E Iceland
  (b) Gulf of Mexico
  (c) Canaries
  (d) Benguela; S Atlantic

B 1 (a) Hebron; (b) No
  2 (a) Portland; (b) Biarritz
  3 (a) Winter is colder on the N American coast
    (b) (i) Europe has warm N Atlantic Drift
      (ii) Cold Labrador current off American coast

Unit 13

A (a) snow and ice
  (b) skis

B (a) No opportunities for work or modern living
  (b) Ground is frozen solid; climate is difficult for men to work in
  (c) Near Russia
  (d) Traditional way of life; scenery; midnight sun
  (e) Very short cool summer; midges and insects in summer

Unit 14

(b) Chipboard – board made from small pieces of wood compressed to make a single block or board
  Plywood – strong thin board made by glueing layers of wood together
  Pit props – short lengths of strong timber used in coal mines to support the roof rocks underground.

B Table 14.1
  Taiga forest in region
  Roads and rivers
  Hydro-electricity stations on R Indals
  R Indals
  Sea or rail

C (a) July; (b) February; (c) 4; (d) 9°C;
  (e) July, August; (f) summer

Unit 15

A (a) (i) Odessa (ii) June (iii) summer (iv) yes
  (v) further east so the climate is more continental
  (b) (i) Astrakhan (ii) 3 (iii) Astrakhan (iv) climate is more continental

B (a) (i) crops which are raw materials for industries
  (ii) tobacco
  (iii) over half the ploughed land in Russia is sown with grain

Unit 16

A (c) Yes – mountains, Vesuvius, island of Capri, old fishing village, good walks

B (a) (i) to enable you to compare a familiar climate with the figures for the resort (ii) October (iii) the rainfall
  (b) (ii) No, short time lag before peak sea water temperature is reached
  (iv) Temperatures and sunshine hours increase appreciably in May and decrease sharply after October

Unit 18

A (d) There is little land suitable for farming
  (e) It dries quicker because the wind blows through it
  (f) Winter feed for animals

Unit 19

A (a) Mediterranean crops are confined to the southern half of Europe. Vines will grow further north than oranges, lemons and olives. Olives grow on the southern coastlands of Mediterranean Europe

  (b) 6
  (c) Olives

B (a) There is no milking parlour
  (b) They do not have many cows
  (c) Winter feed
  (d) Sugar beet; vegetables
  (e) Olive oil; grapes
  (f) Higher standard of living in towns

Unit 20

A (a) Dry farming is practised
  (b) For animal food, beer
  (c) Plenty of rainfall

B (a) Italy (b) Denmark (c) Italy, France, Belgium, Fed Rep Germany

C (a) High negative relationship (b) (ii)

D (a) USSR; (b) (i) Climate is unsuitable (ii) Oats will grow in a cool damp climate (iii) Its climate and soils suit wheat growing (iv) Rye is grown in cool conditions where wheat and barley cannot be grown

Unit 21

B (a) Rectangular and square (b) 5 (c) Shelter from winds
  (d) They were laid out on an empty land

C (a) Storm seas are higher (b) Below sea level
  (c) Enclosing dams, canals and pumping stations (d) To drain away the water (e) The dam which separates the new land from the sea and encloses (protects) it

D H, B, C, E, F, D, G, A

Unit 22

A (a) Because the collective farm crops do not belong to him so he grows his own food (b) An agreed number of days work (c) Because they do not have their own farms

B (a) Community hall, cinema, health centre etc
  (b) For the machinery to get to the more distant parts of the farm
  (c) Fruit, vegetables, flowers
  (d) (i) Grain and sugar beet are grown (ii) To harvest grain (iii) To transport the produce to collecting points (iv) Suits mechanized farming

Unit 23

A (a) A grain (oats); B grain (rye); C sugar beet and potatoes; D grass for hay
  (b) Food for animals (c) Sugar beet, potatoes, grain
  (d) Permanent grass fields

B (a) Cereals; grains and green fodder (b) Clover
  (c) Oats, rye (d) A crop that is grown mainly for its root, for use as food for humans or animals e.g. turnips

Unit 24

A 1 UK 2 Rep Ireland (Eire) 3 Denmark
  4 Fed Rep Germany 5 Netherlands 6 Belgium
  7 Luxembourg 8 France 9 Italy 10 Greece
  11 Spain 12 Portugal

B (a) A (b) B (c) C

C (c) Limits their profits (d) Baby food, food for Third World countries, used in catering (cooking)

Unit 25

A (a) Fed Rep Germany (b) More (c) Rep Ireland (Eire) (d) Netherlands

C (a) (i) Switzerland (ii) Italy (iii) Ireland, Spain

Unit 26

A (a) A and B (b) E and F (c) D (d) E and F

B (b) 55-year-old woman

D (a) The 'pull' of the industrial cities
(b) The capital city acts like a magnet (pull); people leave the poor rural areas (push)
(c) There is a great deal of highland

Unit 27

A (a) (i) European workers did not have far to travel
(ii) They had the skills needed in Germany
(b) Australia has a high standard of living and needs its own workers; the journey from Australia is long and expensive; Australians speak English so there is a language barrier
(c) Pakistan, Bangladesh

B (b) reasons (2) and (3) (c) In the 'others' category
(d) Language barrier, until recently work could be found at home; British emigrant workers prefer to go to Commonwealth countries

Unit 28

A (a) C (b) A

B (b) Farmers make a better living (c) Old ways of life disappear

Unit 29

A (a) A (b) D (c) B

B (b) Industrial activities are concentrated in one region; firms can link up easily; industries can use port facilities.
(c) Advantage : noise is kept away from the city centre
 Disadvantage : travel delay from airport to Hamburg CBD and industrial areas

Unit 30

A (a) South axis – Mantes Sud, Trappes Nord Ouest, Trappes Sud Est, Evry and Tigery Lieusaint
North axis – Cergy, Beauchamp, Bry-sur-Marne/Noisy-le-Grande
(b) To avoid noise and traffic problems (c) 6
(d) Recreation (e) A long way to the city centre; no community spirit at first

B (a) Renewing an out of date part of a town or city
(b) People can get to work easily; convenient for shoppers;
(c) Traffic noise

C (b) Both cities are old and suffer from traffic congestion
(c) Re-houses people from the city; reduces the amount of commuting; diverts industrial traffic from the chief city

Unit 31

C (a) 4, 7 (b) Separates people from traffic; attractive to tourists, removes noise and pollution from the city centre
(c) Deliveries to the shops can be a problem; car drivers cannot park near shops
(e) Land would be made available for a fast inner ring road and for other developments
(f) Easy to find your way around the city; easy to get around the main sights

Unit 33

A (a) 1 Mont Blanc; 2 St Bernard; 3 Brenner
(b) 1 France; 2 Switzerland; 3 Austria
(c) 900 km

D There are various routes, e.g. Florence – Bologna – Turin (Italy) Lyon – Dijon – Calais (France)
Only Switzerland is not a member of the EEC

Unit 34

A (a) East of Paris (b) (ii) radial, like the spokes of a wheel

C (a) (i) 2 hrs 48m (ii) 3 hrs 31m (iii) 3 hrs 12m
(iv) 3 hrs 42m (v) 4 hrs 40m (vi) 4 hrs 45m
(b) (i) 26 (ii) 22 (iii) 16

Unit 35

A (a) London, Paris, Frankfurt, Rome, Amsterdam, Copenhagen, Zurich, Düsseldorf, Munich, Milan
(b) London, Paris, Rome, Copenhagen
(c) They have high populations and are centres of business and administration

B (a) 15.7 km (b) (i) The person living near the airport would be in favour of the new site.
(ii) The businessman would only be in favour if the journey to the airport took less time
(iii) The farmer would not be in favour unless he hoped to sell his land at a high price and did not mind farming elsewhere

C Frankfurt is central in W Germany. It is at the junction of N – S routes. It is close to important motorways, near large industrial and business centres and has a rail link with the airport.

Unit 36

A (a) Stockholm (b) Norrköping (c) 150 km
(d) Via Stockholm and Luleå or via Stockholm direct
(e) Växjö, Stockholm, Norrköping

B (a) Between Vasteras and Ostersund or Ostersund and Kiruna
(b) West and south-west of Stockholm

C (a) Helsinki, Stockholm, Copenhagen, Oslo
(b) Copenhagen (c) Finland (d) The Sound which separates Copenhagen from Malmö slows the journey time

D Switzerland; Belgium; USSR; Netherlands; W Germany; Finland; Italy; Portugal; Poland; Spain

Unit 37

A (a) (ii) 1 Po; 2 Rhône-Saône; 3 Seine;
4 Moselle; 5 Rhine; 6 Neckar; 7 Main;
8 Danube; 9 Albert Canal; 10 Dortmund-Ems Canal; 11 Mittelland Canal; 12 North Sea Canal;
13 Weser; 14 Elbe; 15 Kiel Canal
(b) Rhine – Saône – Rhône; Moselle – Rhône – Saône; Main – Danube (c) New, deeper waterways would encourage more north-south trade and in the case of the Main – Danube, make better trade links between Western and Eastern Europe

C (a) The Netherlands is a low, flat country, well-suited to waterways. It is also at the mouth of the river Rhine. Britain is more hilly, has few suitable rivers and canals. (b) Oil, chemicals, gas (c) carrying goods by air (d) The table is based on the weight of the goods. Goods carried by air would be a very small proportion of the total on this basis (e) Perishable and valuable goods which are relatively light-weight

Unit 38

A (b) Netherlands; France; Belgium; W Germany (c) Poland (d) 87.5 million tonnes

B (a) The channel and docks are too small and shallow for large supertankers. There is not enough land available for oil refinery building. (b) Good rail communications; on New Waterway; land space for warehouses etc (c) Possibly an oil refinery, chemical processing works or a food processing plant

Unit 39

A (b) The south (c) 100 km (d) River Meuse

B (a) To avoid the residential and industrial suburbs (b) (i) A pedestrian precinct would attract customers and improve the environment (ii) the fly-over would spoil the historic area of the old city and drive tourists away (iii) Banning cars might drive away more customers unless suitable city transport was introduced to encourage people into the city centre (iv) Old buildings attract tourists. Knocking down old buildings to make way for a multi-storey car park is not going to bring more tourists to your restaurant.

C (a) The main differences are: commuters use more private cars and rail transport than school pupils; they use less trams/buses and two-wheeled vehicles. (b) Commuters tend to travel longer distances to work than pupils going to school. They therefore use rail services more frequently and can drive their own cars. Pupils will have short journeys and will use trams/buses and bicycles to get to school.

Unit 40

A (a) Air freight – for speed, safety (b) Water transport via the Rhine and Neckar because stone is heavy and bulky (c) By road or rail because the clocks are fairly light and can travel in containers (d) By rail because the machinery is heavy and must be hauled across the Alps (e) By road because the cheese will deteriorate fairly quickly and rail services are likely to be slower

B (a) (ii) By road – Basel, Frankfurt, Milan, Zurich
By rail – Amsterdam, Belgrade, Berlin, Hamburg, Hanover
By road or rail – Cologne
(b) (i) £300 (ii) £350 (c) £25 (£250 − £225)

Unit 41

A (a) 7 (b) 90 (c) 6 (d) 5 (e) 60° N (f) 1200 km

B (a) Kiruna, Gällivare, Svappavaara (b) Kiruna is well within the Arctic Circle and during much of the winter the sun never rises above the horizon, or the amount of daylight is very short.

C (c)

E Kiruna is too remote: labour and transport costs would be very high; climatic conditions are difficult. Grängesberg is in the more populated part of Sweden with transport costs less and climatic conditions better.

Unit 42

A (a) 20 (b) 2 (c) Fos, Zelzate (d) There has been a shift towards coastal locations

B (a) Denmark + 60 per cent; W Germany − 32.8 per cent; France − 31.9 per cent; Italy + 3.8 per cent; Netherlands − 41.4 per cent; UK − 38.6 per cent (b) Belgium/Luxembourg (c) Denmark, Italy

C (a) The Ruhr, Lorraine, Sweden (b) Waterways – Rhine and canals (c) (i) On the North Sea with deep water quays in works (ii) At the end of the North Sea Canal (iii) On the North Sea leading to the New Waterway (d) Probably by road or rail

Unit 43

A (a) Over 70 per cent of Western Europe's oil comes from the Persian Gulf or countries around the Mediterranean.
(b) Tankers from the Persian Gulf do not have to travel into the Atlantic and North Sea so the journey is shorter.
(c) The demand for petrol and other oil products is highest in densely populated areas.

B (a) River Rhône
(b) Iran, Iraq, Kuwait, Saudi Arabia, Qatar, United Arab Emirates
(c) Via the Suez Canal or via the Cape of Good Hope
(d) Egypt, Libya (e) Raw materials can be obtained from the oil refineries (f) Deep water; suitable land available; easy access to Middle East supplies; good inland routes including the pipeline

Unit 44

A (b) A – railway tracks and sidings; B – main road; C – factories; D – town centre; E – housing; F – farmland; G – coal mines; H – graveyard; I – woodland
(c) No, industry, housing and other facilities are haphazard

B Heavy industry; industries using products of heavy industry; market located industries; service industries; industrial region or core area

Unit 45

A (a) The market for finished goods is in the big cities. Many materials and accessories are made in core areas.
(b) The large population of the area provides a market and the skilled workers needed.
(c) The main market is the service industries of the core area. Labour is also available.
(d) The market for bottles is the firms producing food products and liquids such as beer. These are mainly located in core areas where there is a market for the products.

B (a) Car exhausts can add to smog.
(b) Smoke from the chimneys creates smog.
(c) Smog can be very dangerous to health, especially for people with breathing problems.
(d) Acid rain from sulphur dioxide; water pollution from discharging waste into rivers; dumping factory waste materials

D (c) The automobile industry; domestic appliance industries, e.g. washing machines

Unit 46

A (a) Distance to market is greater
(b) There is more competition for labour in a core area than in a remote region
(c) Because the government would pay 60 per cent
(d) At Doëlan, by 30 000 francs
(e) 360 000 francs
(f) Doëlan, by 240 000 francs

B (b) (i) Approve – more clients (ii) Might approve – more customers, but might regret not having a fish factory instead (iii) Approve – work for children and possibly herself (iv) Might disapprove – concern about effect on tourist trade, but more trade from increase in population

Unit 47

A (a) Walking, climbing, bird-watching etc
(b) Tobogganing, ice skating, discos
(c) As ski slopes
(d) By cable car or chair lift
(e) December, January, February, March, when temperatures are below zero
(f) Mild, 13°C, some rain 125 mm in month.

B (d) Some lines are very thin compared with the line for West Germany which is difficult to fit into the space on the map.

Unit 48

A (a) 2 – a health hazard and looks unpleasant;
3 – unpleasant for sunbathers and swimmers;
4 – decrease in farmland, land prices increase, alter character of the area;
5 – Noise and air pollution, risk of accidents;
6 – congestion, restricts turtles breeding in the area;
7 – noise pollution;
8 – change in character of shops, shopkeepers may not be interested in needs of local people;
9 – dying out of old customs and traditions or changing them to meet the needs of the visitors
(b) Plan development carefully; keep beaches clean; make people aware of dangers to the environment; improve rubbish disposal; control nightclubs with licenses; close centre of Zákinthos town to cars; control noise and speeding

B (b) After falling rapidly, the population loss has slowed down.
(c) The rate of change has altered, population loss almost stopped between 1971 and 1981
(d) The slowing down is due to more jobs being available from the tourist industry.

C (a) The best months are May, June and September when rainfall is low and temperatures are not too high.

Glossary

atmospheric pressure The weight the atmosphere exerts on the surface of the earth. At sea level this atmospheric pressure is 1013.5 millibars on average.

chernozem A black or dark brown rich soil. It is found in the continental grasslands which stretch from Manchuria (China) through the USSR to Hungary and Romania. It is a fertile soil famous for its use to produce cereals.

commercial farming Farming which is concerned mainly with producing crops and animal products for sale, rather than with producing food for the farmer and his family.

condensation The changing of a gas (e.g. water vapour) into its liquid form (e.g. water). In the atmosphere this happens either when moist air is cooled or when the air becomes saturated.

continental climates The climates found in the interiors of continents. They are characterized by low rainfall and large daily and yearly ranges in temperature. Summers are warm and winters cold, with most rain falling in summer.

contour A line on a map which joins all points of the same height above sea level.

convection A process of heat transference within the atmosphere or within a gas or fluid. Liquids and gases expand and rise when heated, forming convection currents.

converging plates Plates of the earth's crust that are drifting towards one another (see diverging plates).

cooperative farming A system of farming, in which a group of farmers join together to get greater economic benefits than they could get on their own.

core area The industrial and urban region in which economic progress has reached its peak, in contrast with other areas, known as the periphery, which are less well developed (see periphery).

cross-section A diagram which shows the height of the land along a line drawn across a map.

crust The outermost shell of the earth which varies in thickness from about 6 km below the oceans to 60 km under the high mountain regions.

dispersed industries Industries which are scattered, rather than being concentrated into particular regions.

diverging plates Plates of the earth's crust that are drifting away from one another (see converging plates).

drought A period of dry weather which is long enough for the vegetation to begin to wilt. In Britain an absolute drought is a period of at least fifteen consecutive days when less than 0.25 mm of rainfall is experienced each day.

dry farming A type of farming used in semi-arid lands to catch and store moisture in the ground so that crops can be grown. Usually crops are grown every other year, and in the fallow year the surface is broken up so that moisture can be conserved for the next year's crop.

earth's axis The imaginary line running through the centre of the earth connecting the North Pole with the South Pole.

emigrant A person who has left his/her native country and has settled permanently in another.

enrichment A process whereby waste material is removed from an ore to make the ore purer.

entrepôt port A port that deals mainly with the distribution of goods to other places by transferring them from ocean-going ships to barges or vice-versa.

evaporation The process whereby a liquid (e.g. water), is changed into a gas (water vapour). Evaporation from the earth provides most of the water vapour in the atmosphere, which in turn influences most types of weather.

free port A port into which goods can be brought without customs duties being paid, if the goods are to be processed or packaged for export.

geest An area of heathland which has infertile, coarse, sand and gravel soils. Geest lands are found in Denmark, the Netherlands and NW Germany.

gross domestic product (GDP) The total value of goods and services produced by a country in one year.

high grade iron ore Ore with over 50 per cent iron content.

humidity The amount of water vapour present in the atmosphere.

immigrant A person who is not a native of the country in which he/she is now settled.

industrial inertia The tendency for firms and industries to remain in a particular location after the original causes for choosing that location have disappeared, e.g. the Sheffield steel industry.

latitude An imaginary line drawn round the Earth parallel to the Equator. Lines of latitude are measured as distances north and south of the Equator in degrees from 0° to 90°. They are sometimes called parallels.

lean iron ore An ore with a low percentage of iron, usually between 30% and 50%.

longitude An imaginary line running north – south at right angles to the parallels. Lines of longitude are numbered from 0° to 180° east and west of the 0° Prime Meridian. They are sometimes called meridians.

ocean current The movement of a mass of water from one part of the ocean to another. Currents moving towards the Poles are generally warm currents, currents moving towards the Equator are cold currents.

park and ride A scheme used in city suburbs to encourage people to park their cars and take bus or train transport into the city centre.

peripheral The adjective derived from periphery (see below). For example, Brittany is one of the peripheral regions to the Paris core area.

periphery The region which is not part of the core area; it is dependent upon, but less well developed than the core area (see core area).

permafrost Permanently frozen ground found in very cold regions. In tundra lands the surface soil thaws out in summer but ground temperatures beneath the surface stay permanently below freezing.

plate A section of the outer shell of the earth which is separated from other sections and 'floats' over the material beneath.

plate margins The edges of plates where earthquakes and volcanoes occur.

podsol (podzol) A soil formed in cool damp climates in areas of heath and coniferous forest. On the surface it has an ash-grey colour but gets darker in colour lower down. This is the typical soil of the taiga region.

polder A piece of land reclaimed from the sea or a lake. When the land has been reclaimed and the salt removed the polder is usually very fertile.

pressure gradient The rate of change of atmospheric pressure between two points on the earth's surface. It is shown on a weather map by the spacing of the isobars. If isobars are close together the gradient is steep and winds are strong.

Prime Meridian The 0° longitude line which runs through Greenwich and is used as the basis for Greenwich Mean Time.

push-barge convoy A number of large barges connected together, which are pushed by another vessel. These convoys are a common sight on the major waterways of Western Europe.

rural depopulation The movement of people away from rural areas such as the Massif Central of France or the Highlands of Scotland.

saeter (seter) A mountain pasture to which cattle are sent during the summer months in Scandinavia. Similar pastures in Switzerland are called 'alps'.

transpiration The loss of water vapour into the air from plants. Generally the higher the air temperature the greater the rate of transpiration.

vertical exaggeration The amount by which the vertical scale on a map is greater than the horizontal scale.

xerophytic These plants can survive long droughts because they are adapted to dry conditions, e.g. by having very long roots, tubers in which to store moisture, leaf structures which cut down transpiration.

zones of dispersal Areas or regions from which people have migrated to more attractive and economically more active regions or cities.